THE VOWEL VAN
GAMES & ACTIVITIES

WRITTEN BY PAM COON * ILLUSTRATED BY BEV ARMSTRONG

THE LEARNING WORKS

The purchase of this book entitles the individual teacher to reproduce copies for use in the classroom.

The reproduction of any part for an entire school or school system or for commercial use is strictly prohibited.

No form of this work may be reproduced or transmitted or recorded without written permission from the publisher.

Copyright © 1980 — THE LEARNING WORKS, INC.
All rights reserved.
Printed in the United States of America.

Notes to the Teacher

The Vowel Van consists of three levels of activities for the long vowels *a e i o u* and three levels of activities for the short vowels *a e i o u*. The long vowels are presented first, but the format is flexible so that you may use the activities in the sequence that best suits the special needs and abilities of your children.

The activities of the Vowel Van will help develop visual and auditory discrimination, eye-hand coordination, and vocabulary. Because these activities are highly motivating, the children will become actively involved in the learning process.

The activities are divided into three levels, progressing from very simple picture activities to more difficult activities that require reading.

> **Level 1** contains cut-and-paste activities that introduce the vowel in the initial position, where it is easiest for the child to hear and to recognize visually. Pictures illustrate words that begin with the vowel sound being presented. Encourage the children to trace the vowel letter outlined on the larger picture and then to say the word represented by each smaller picture as they cut it out and paste it on. The first time or two, you may wish to go over the smaller pictures with the children to avoid any confusion in identifying the objects. Caution them that they will **not** use all of the small pictures each time.
>
> **Level 2** contains cut-and-paste activities that present the vowel sound in the medial position. Pictures illustrate words that contain the vowel sound being studied. As before, encourage the children to trace the vowel letter outlined on the larger picture and then to say the word represented by each smaller picture as they cut it out.
>
> **Level 3** contains manipulative activities that again present the vowel in the medial position. Children now must apply their knowledge of vowel sounds and of initial and final consonants to decode the word. The main support picture reminds them of the vowel sound and of the word family to which it belongs.

Each activity consists of two pages. In general, directions and a large picture appear on the first page, while the second page contains smaller pictures or word wheels to be cut out and pasted or fastened by a brad to the larger picture. To help your children visualize the finished product, the second page often contains a sketch of the completed picture or the assembled word wheel.

For many of the Level 3 activities, two wheels are provided. The first wheel represents a word family that is directly related to the larger object pictured, to which it will be attached. The second wheel is based on the same vowel sound but uses another word family. If you intend to use both wheels simultaneously, you will need to supply a second copy of the large picture for each child.

To make the word wheels more substantial, cut out and glue the picture and the wheels to lightweight tag board. You may even want to laminate one or two for day-after-day class use. Then use pointed scissors where needed to open the "word windows" along the dotted lines, and use a paper punch to make holes for the brad.

Ape

Cut out the bananas that begin with the sound of long a.
Paste them in the ape's hands and feet.

Long a
Level 1

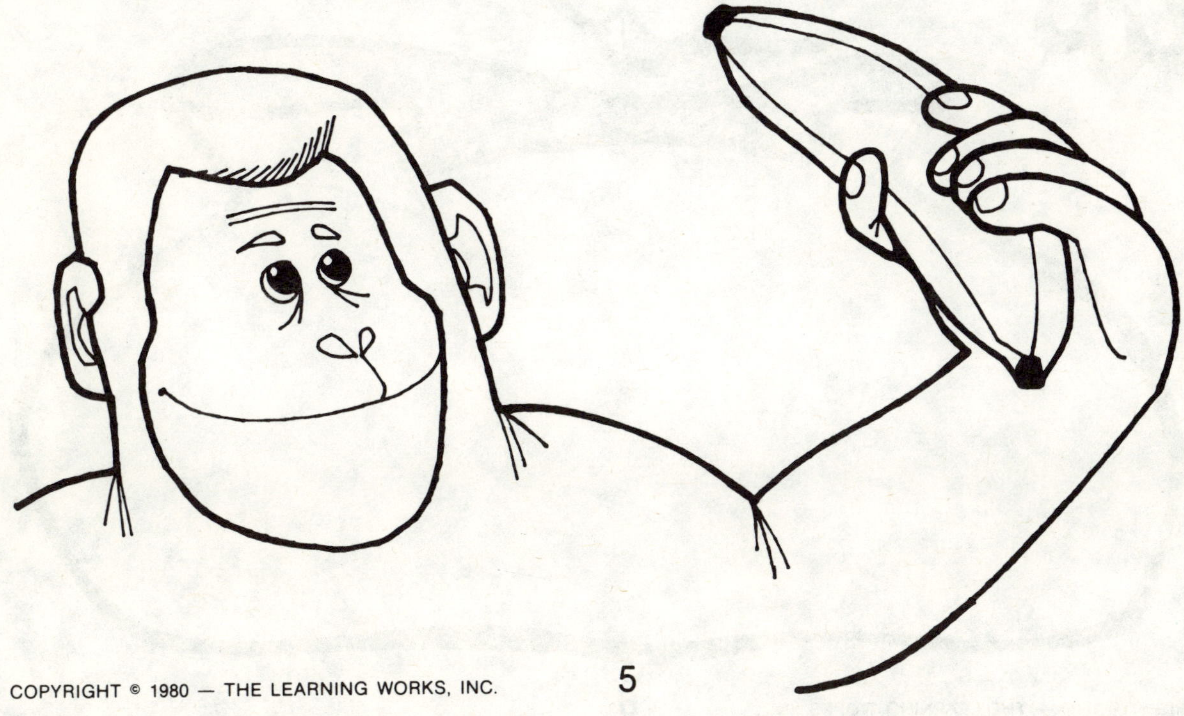

Ape

Long a
Level 2

Acorn

Cut out the acorns that have the long a sound.
Paste them in the squirrel's sack.

Long a
Level 2

Acorn

Cake

Cut out the cake and the wheel. Attach the wheel behind the cake with a brad. Turn the wheel and read the words.

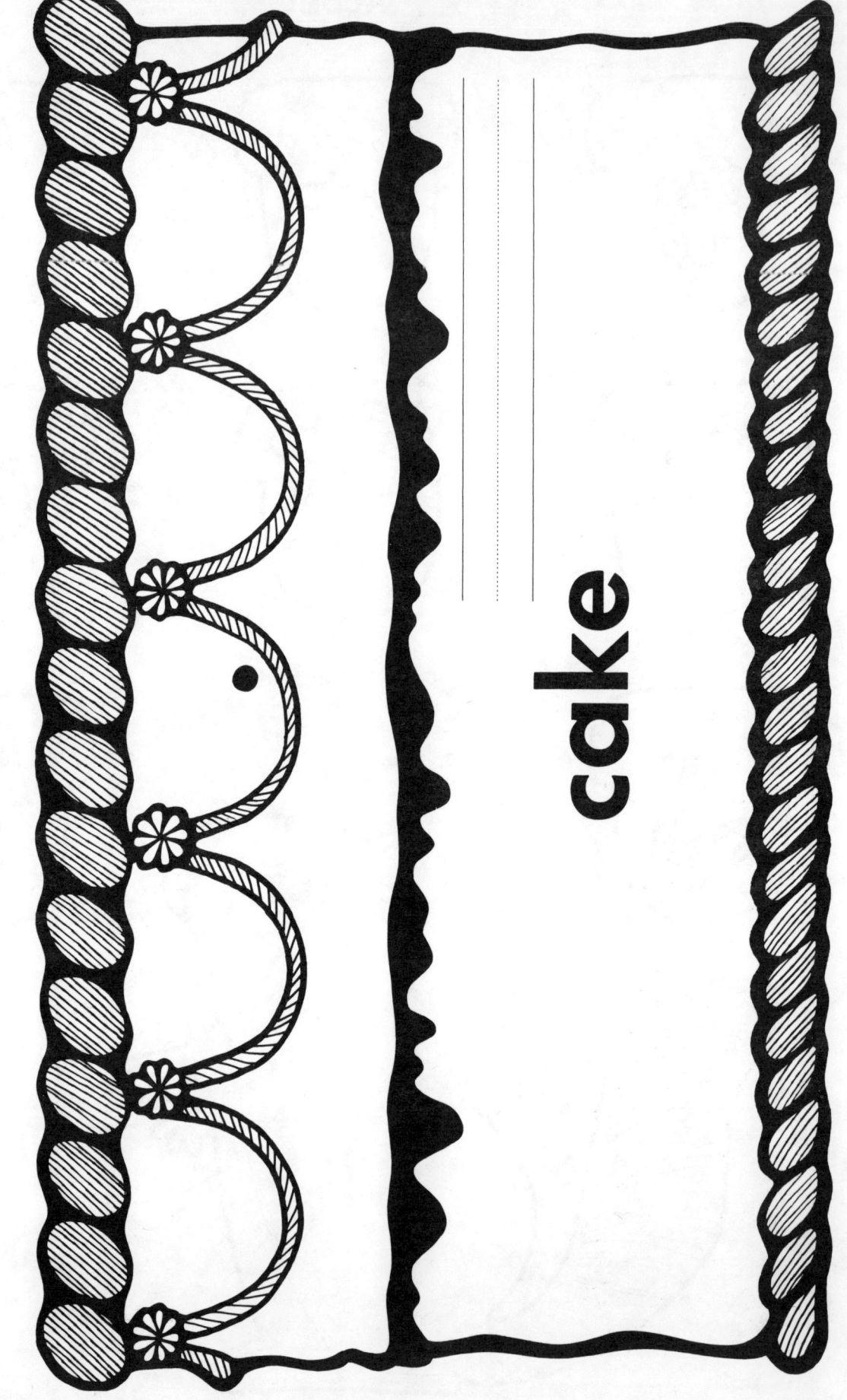

cake

Long a
Level 3

COPYRIGHT © 1980 — THE LEARNING WORKS, INC.

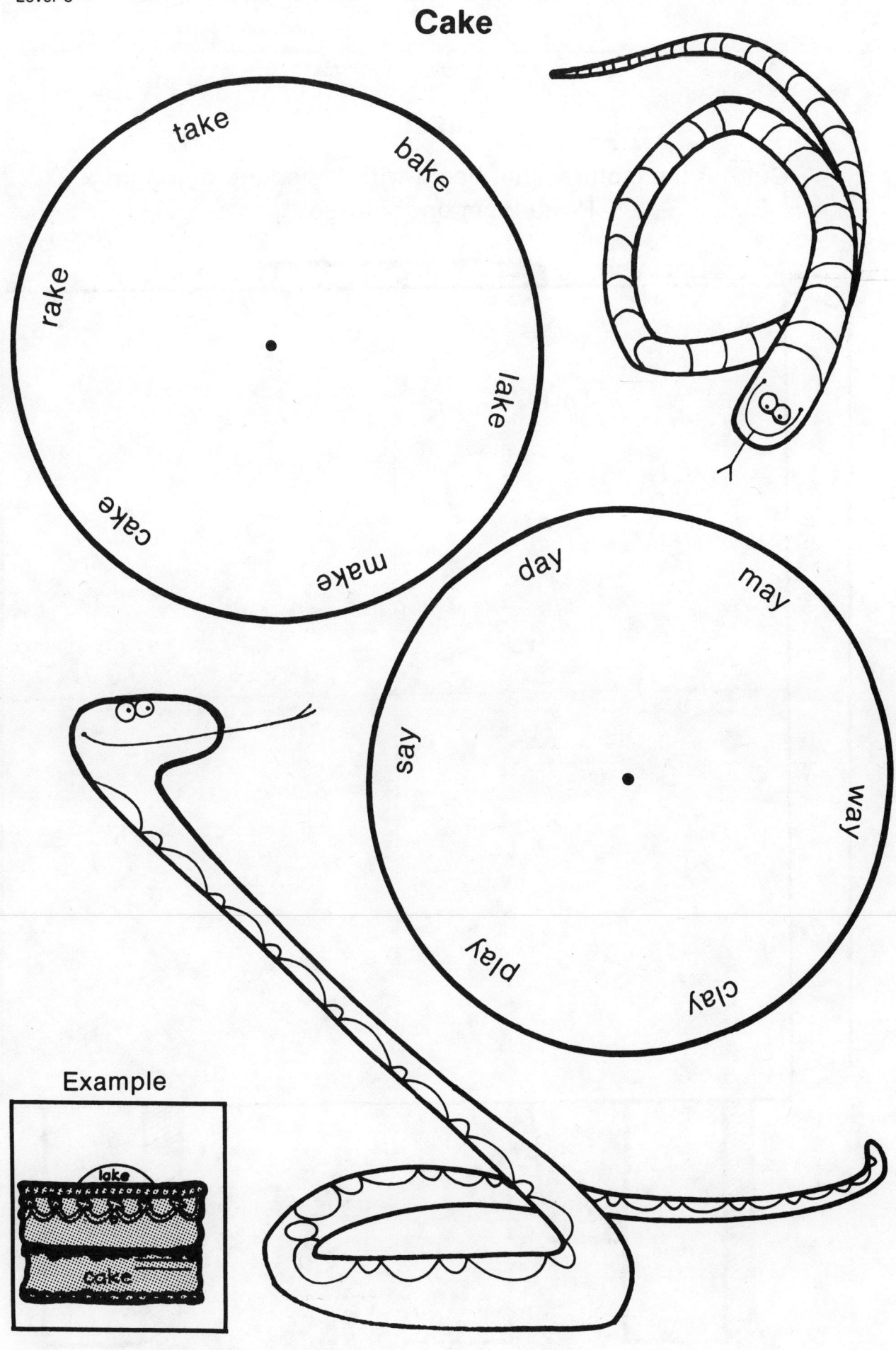

Long e
Level 1

Easel

Cut out the pictures that begin with the sound of long e.
Paste them on the easel.

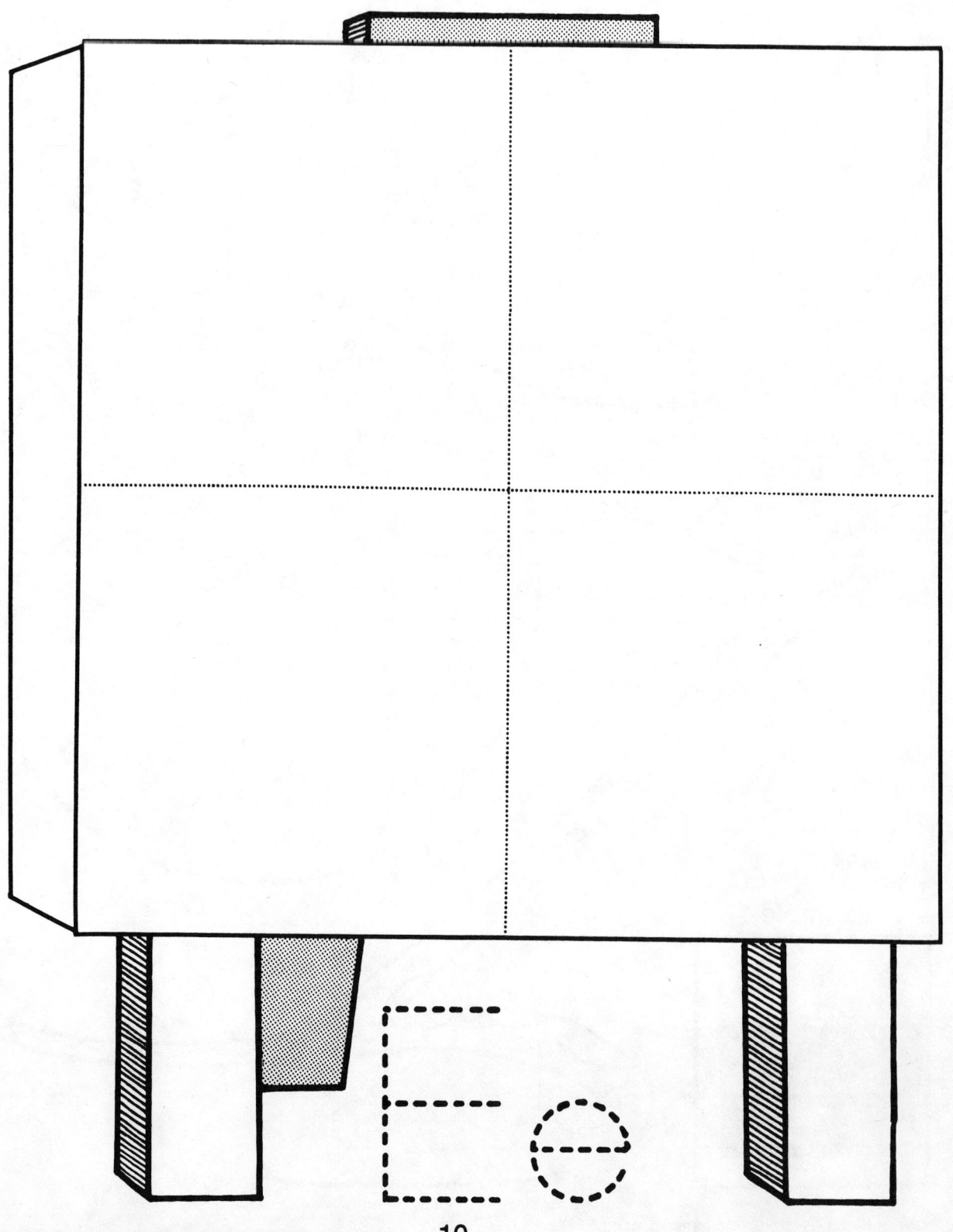

COPYRIGHT © 1980 — THE LEARNING WORKS, INC. 10

Long e
Level 1

Easel

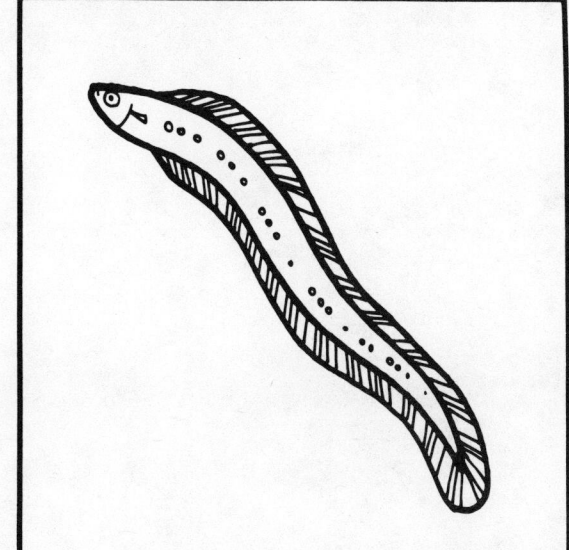

COPYRIGHT © 1980 — THE LEARNING WORKS, INC.

Long 3
Level 2

Eagle

Cut out the clouds that have the sound of long e.
Paste them under the eagle.

Eagle

Long e
Level 3

Wheels

Cut out the van. Cut along the dotted lines of the wheels. Cut out the two wheels on the next page. Attach the wheels behind the van with a brad. Turn the wheels and read the words.

Long e
Level 3

Wheels

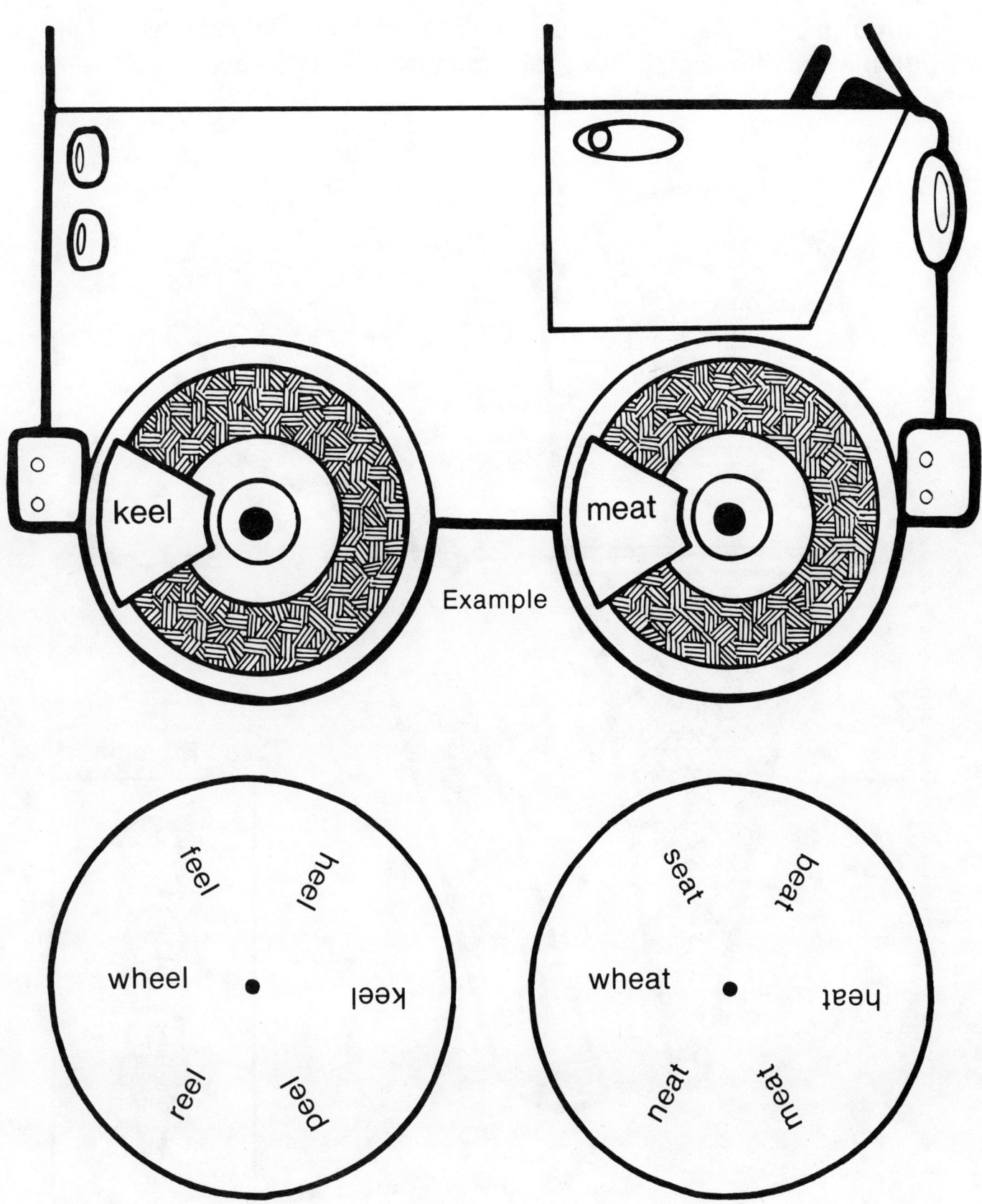

Example

Long i
Level 1

Ice Cream

Cut out the ice cream cone. Cut out the ice cream scoops that begin with the sound of long i. Paste them on the ice cream cone.

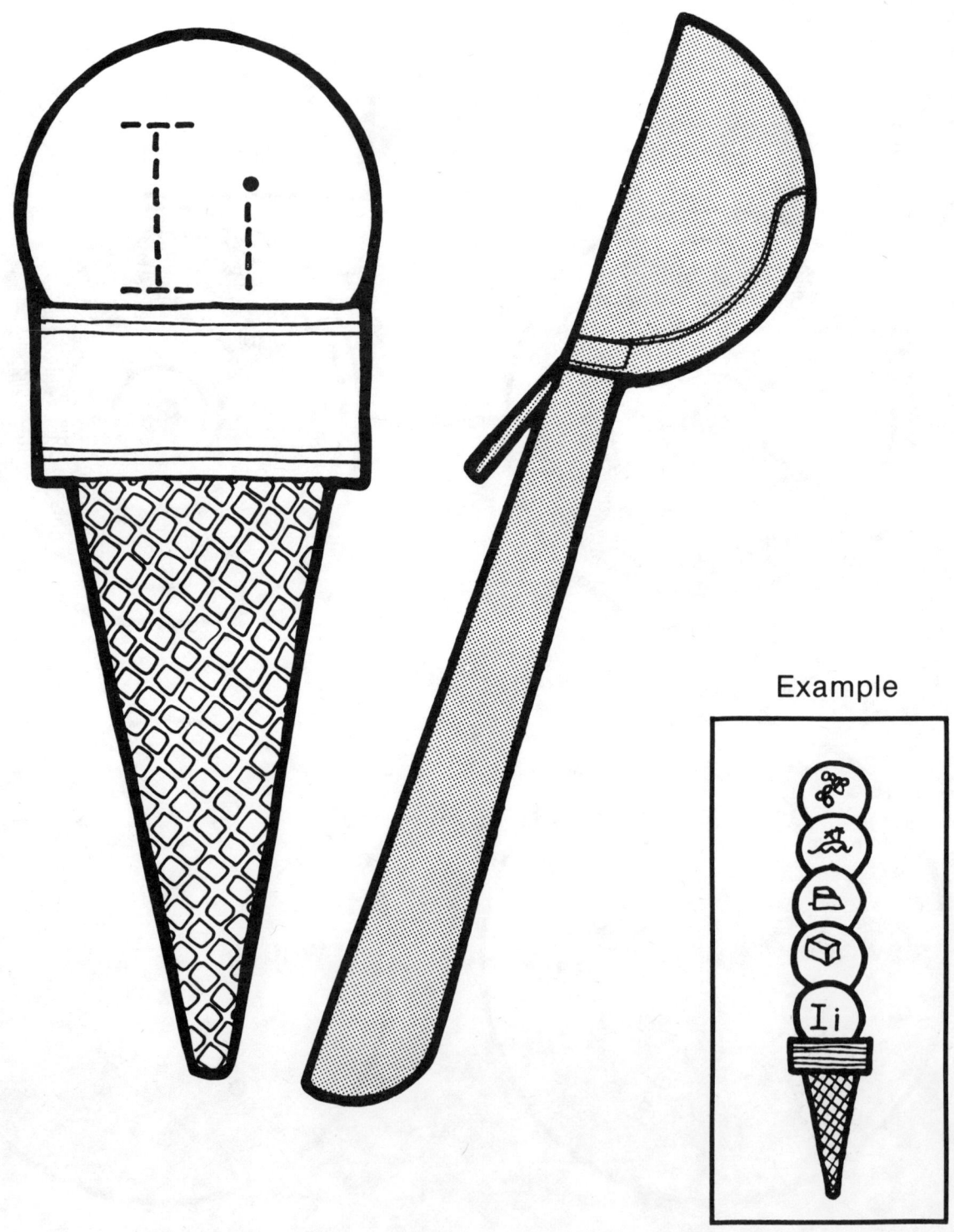

Example

Long i
Level 1

Ice Cream

Long i
Level 2

Icy Drink

Cut out the ice cubes that have the sound of long i. Paste them in the icy drink.

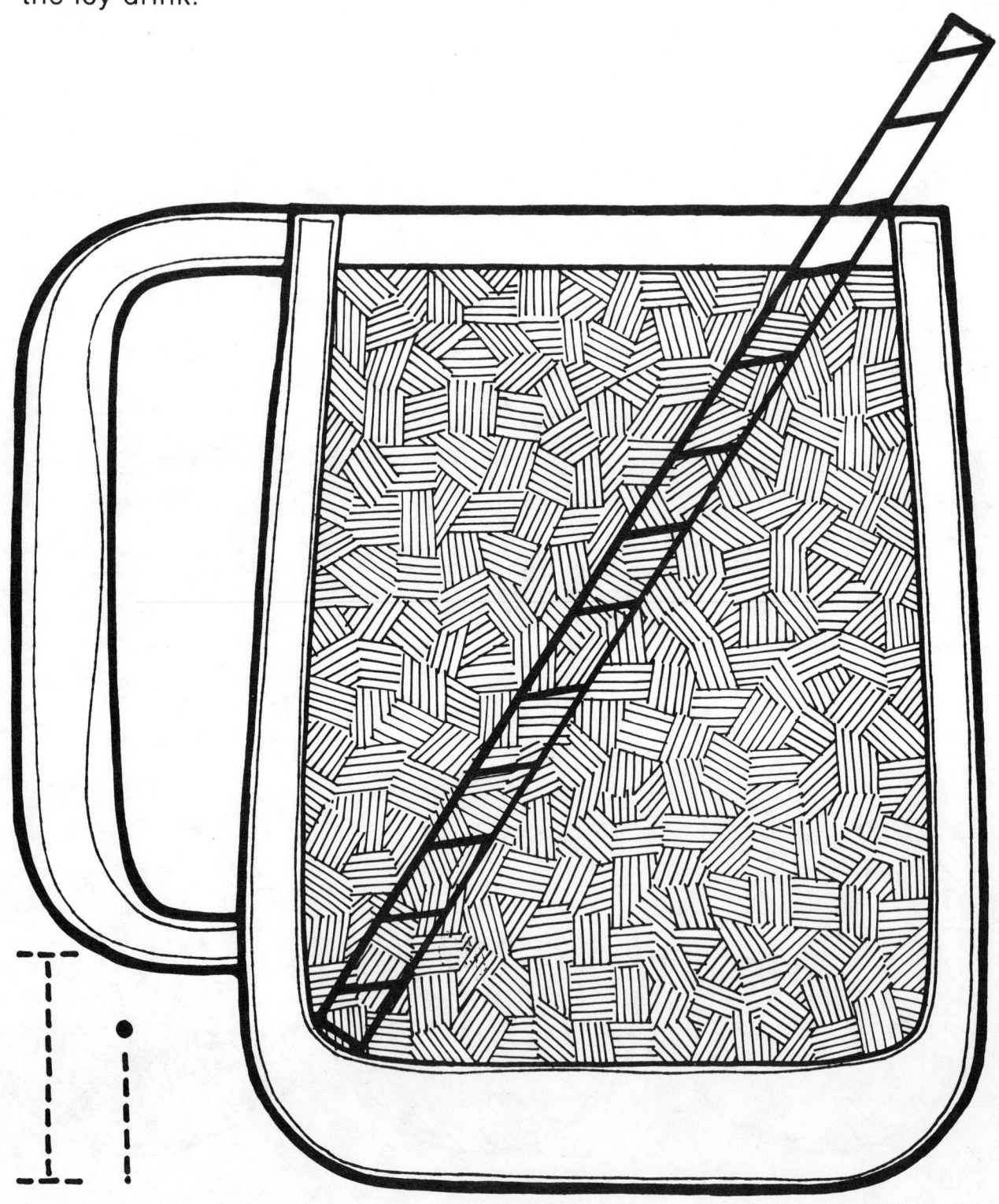

Long i
Level 2

Icy Drink

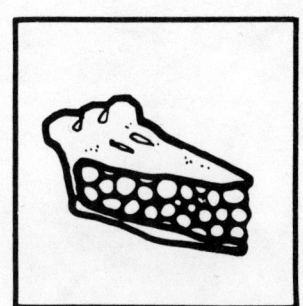

Long i
Level 3

Smile

Cut out the monster's smile. Cut out the wheel and attach it behind the monster's head with a brad. Turn the wheel and read the words.

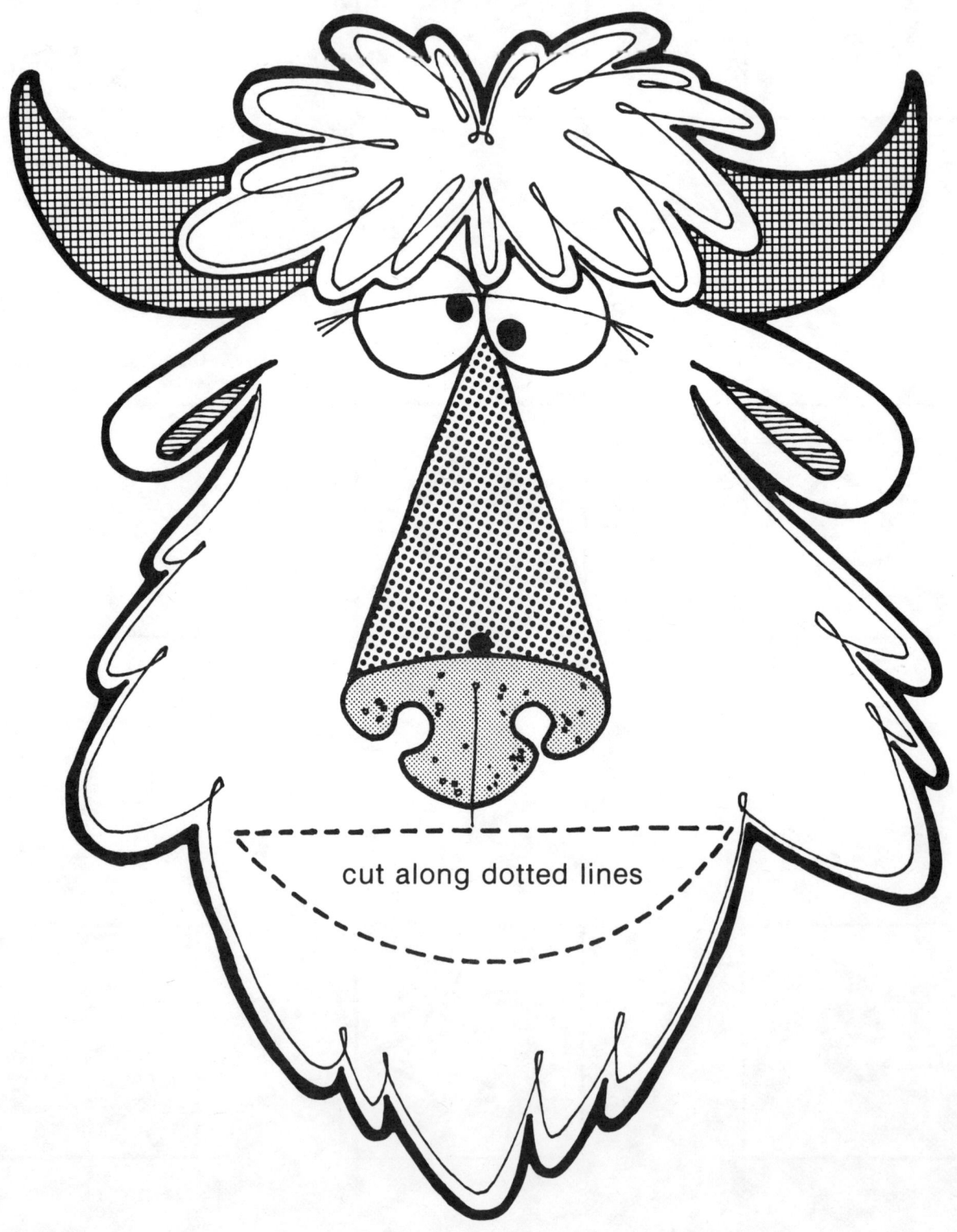

cut along dotted lines

20

COPYRIGHT © 1980 — THE LEARNING WORKS, INC.

Long i
Level 3

Smile

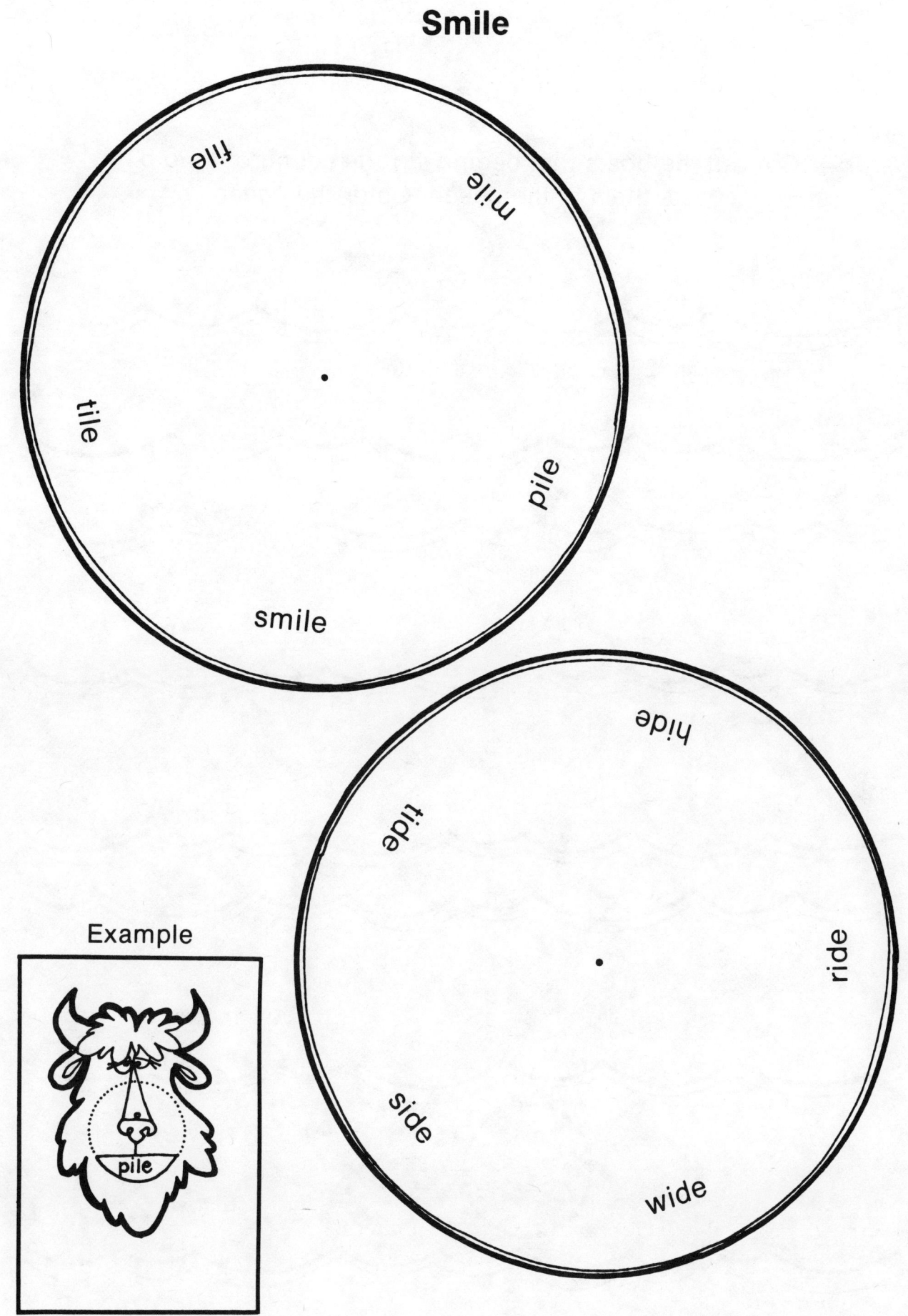

Example

21

Long o
Level 1

Ocean

Cut out the boats that begin with the sound of long o.
Paste them in the ocean. Color the ocean.

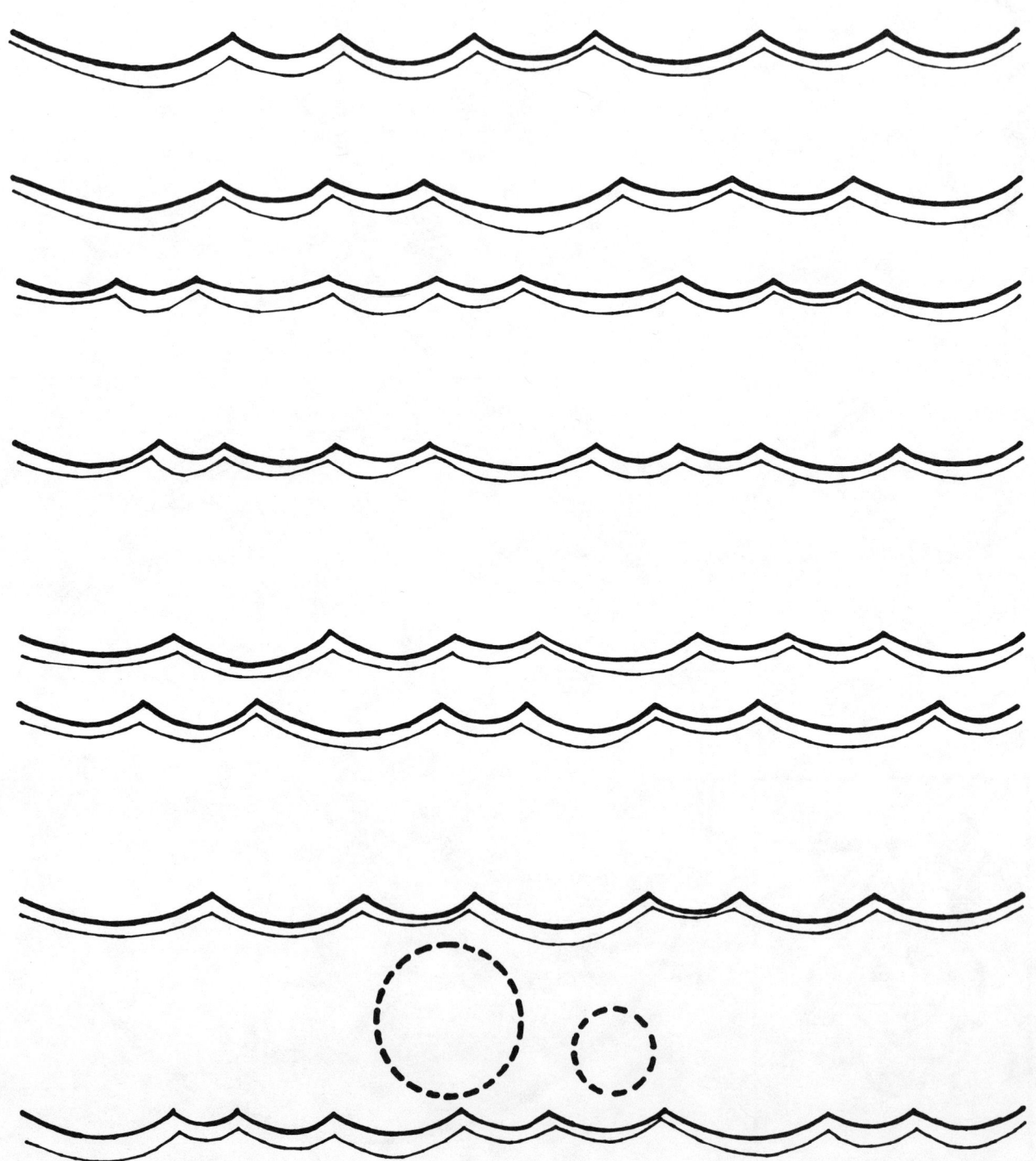

Long o
Level 1

Ocean

23

Long o
Level 2

Old Man

Cut out the strips that have the sound of long o. Paste them on the old man's face to make a beard. Curl the strips around your pencil.

Example

Long o
Level 2

Old Man

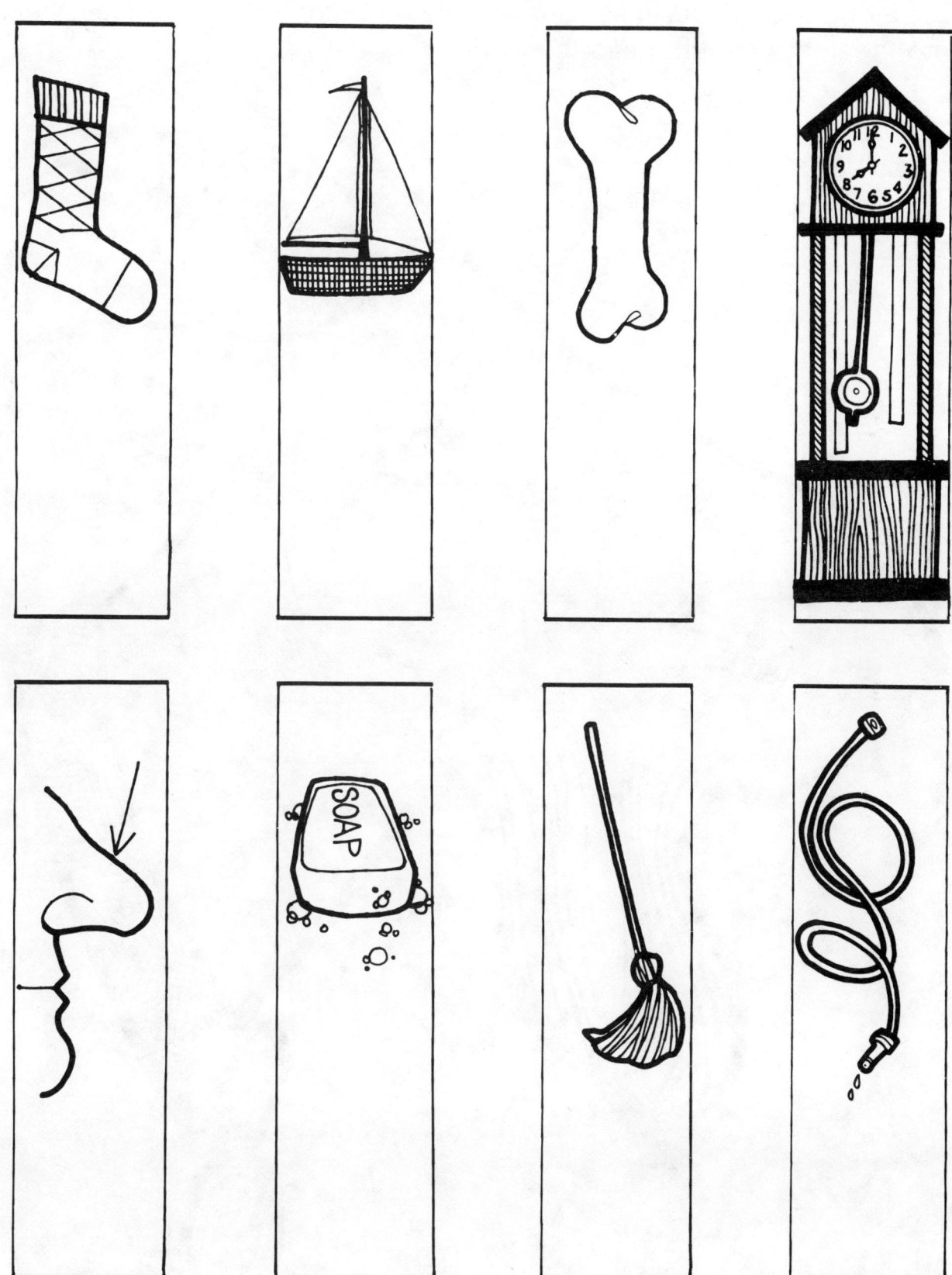

25

Long o
Level 3

Goat

Cut along the dotted lines. Cut out the strips of words and feed them into the goat's mouth. Read the words.

26

Long o
Level 3

Goat

| goat | coat | boat | moat | oat | float |

| cope | hope | rope | dope | lope | mope |

Example

Long u
Level 1

Uniform

Cut out the medals that begin with the sound of long u.
Paste them on the uniform.

Long u
Level 1

Uniform

29

Long u
Level 2

Mule

Cut out the things that have the sound of long u.
Paste them in the mule's pack.

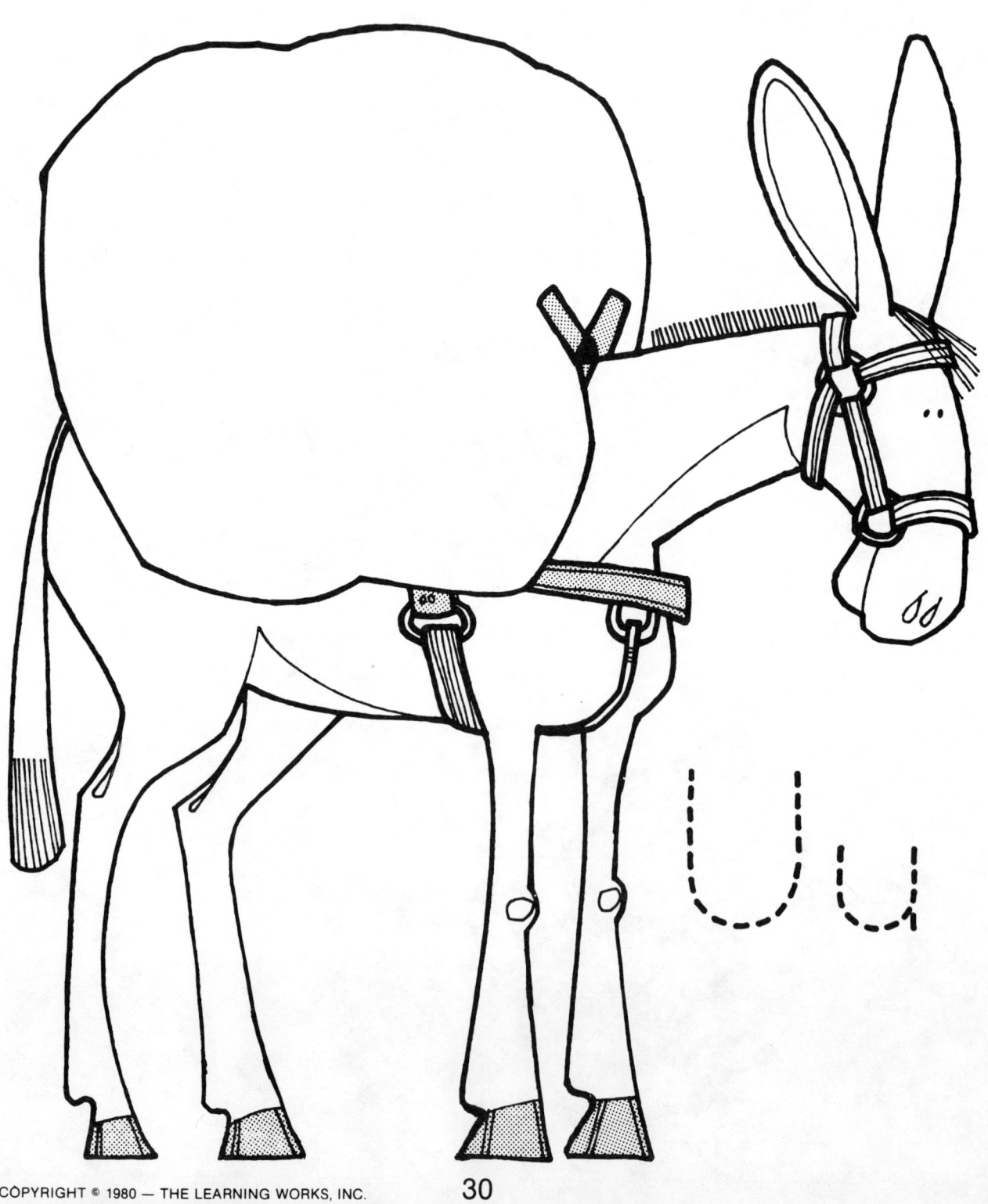

Long u
Level 2

Mule

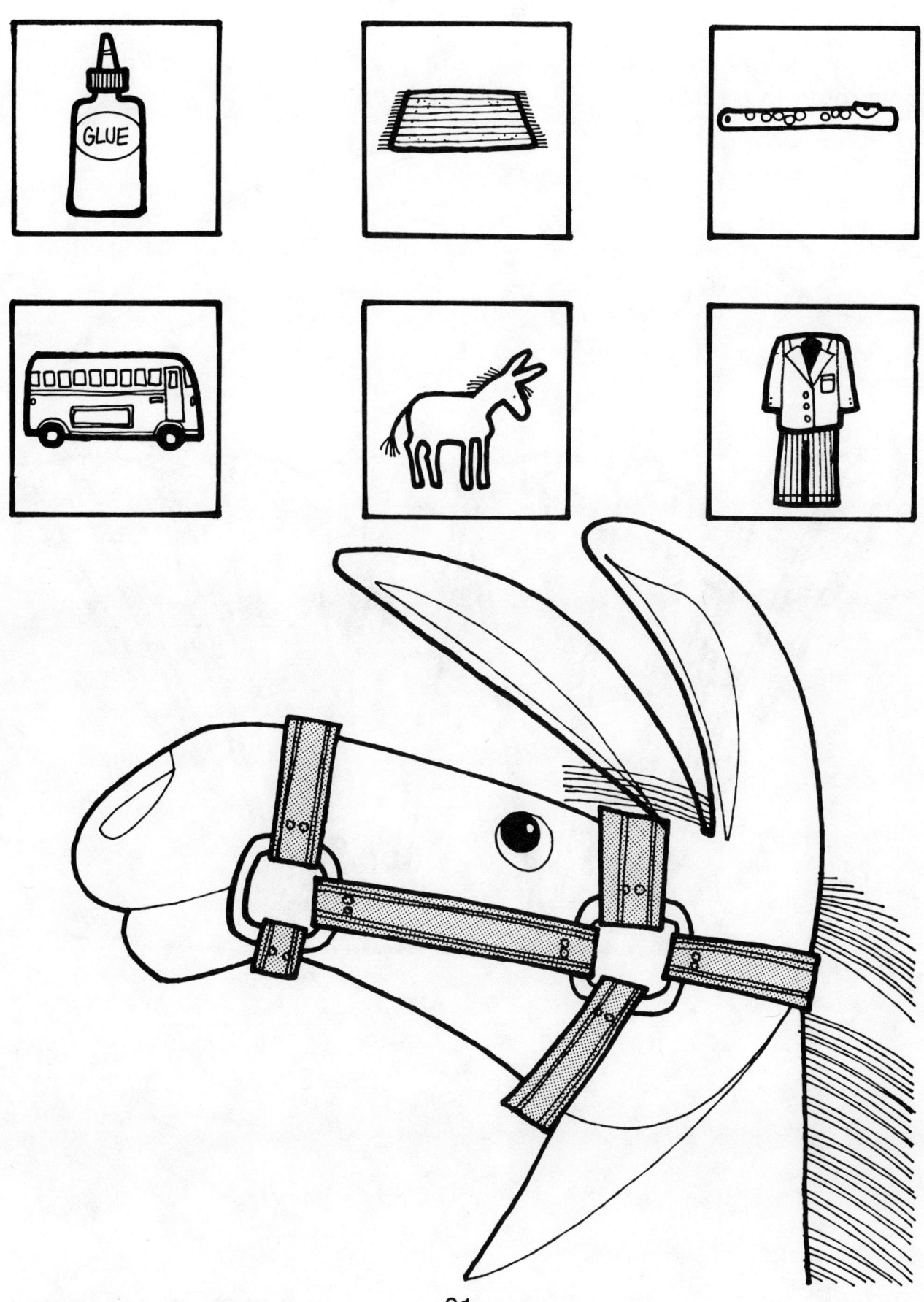

Long u
Level 3

Parachute

Cut out the parachute and the boy. Cut out the list of words. Paste them according to directions on the tabs. Read the words.

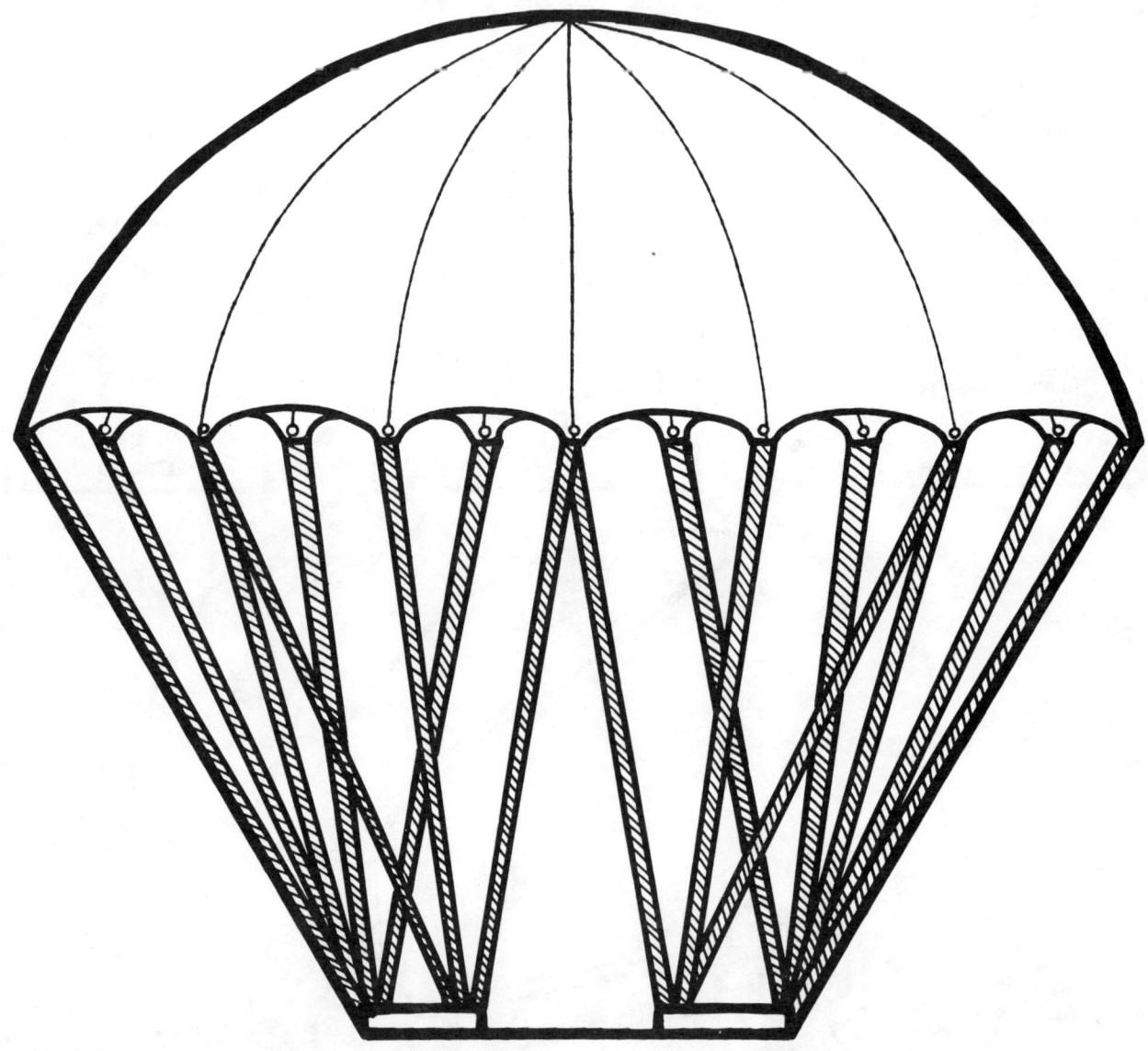

Long u
Level 3

Parachute

Cut along dotted lines.

Paste behind upper portion of parachute.

chute

flute

mute

cute

suit

fruit

Paste behind boy.

Example

COPYRIGHT © 1980 — THE LEARNING WORKS, INC.   33

Short a
Level 1

Aa   **Animal Act**

Cut out the hats that begin with the sound of short a. Paste them on the animals.

COPYRIGHT © 1980 — THE LEARNING WORKS, INC.

34

Short a
Level 1

Animal Act

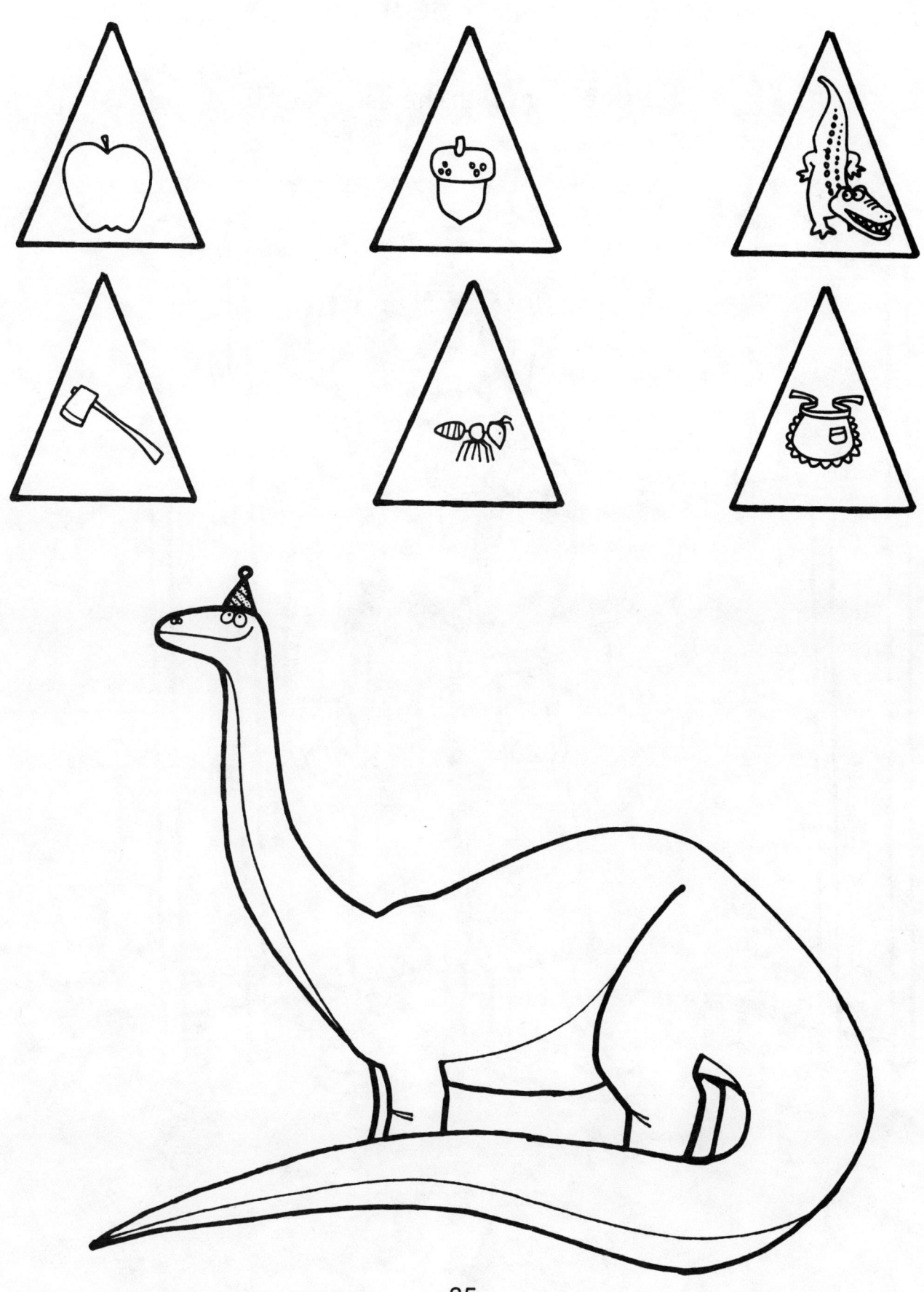

35

Short a
Level 2

Astronaut

Cut out the flags that have the sound of short a.
Paste them with the astronaut.

Short a
Level 2

Astronaut

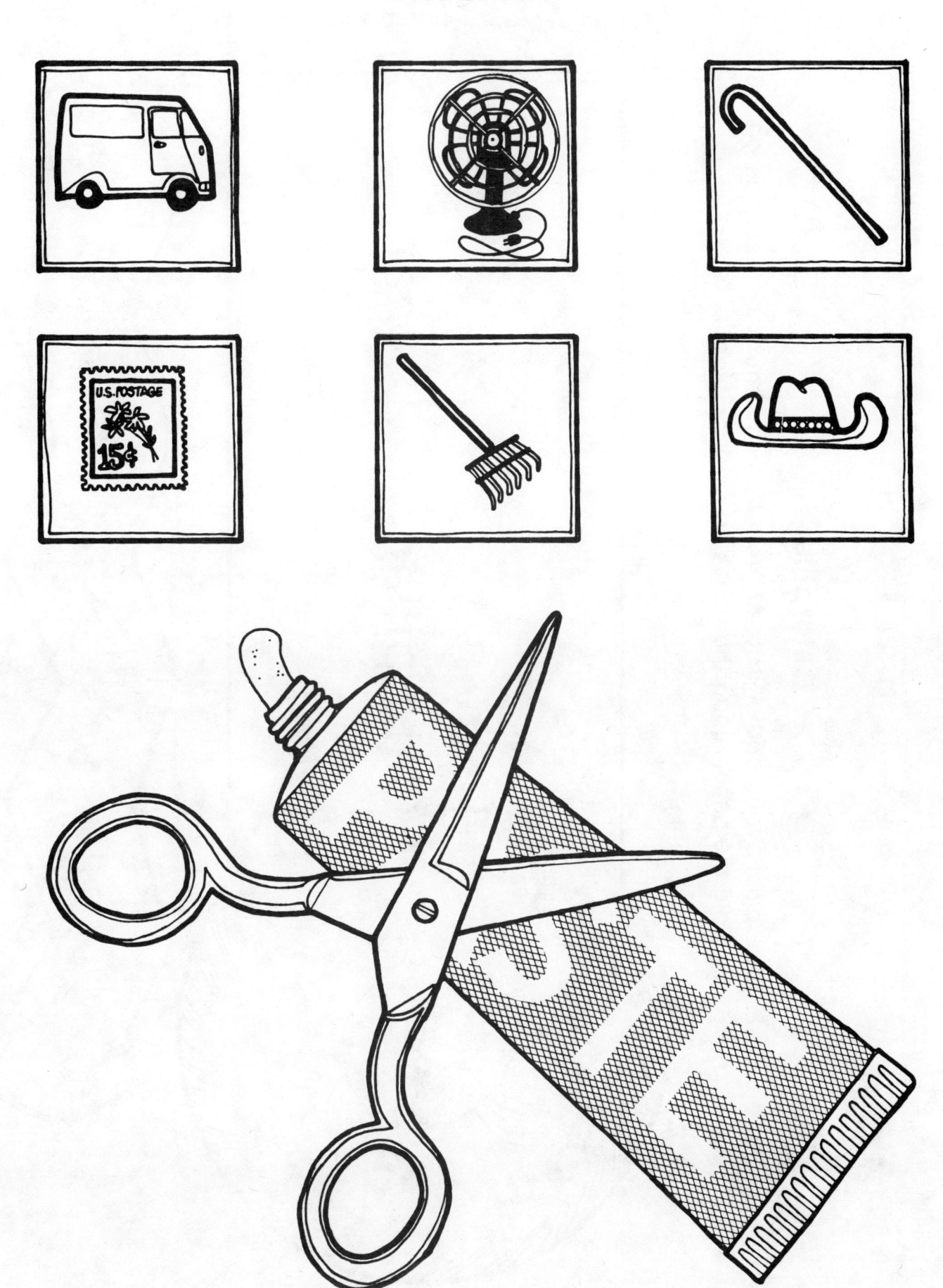

37

COPYRIGHT © 1980 — THE LEARNING WORKS, INC.

Caterpillar

Cut out Patty Caterpillar's long body. Paste her together according to directions on tabs.
Paste her together according to directions on tabs.
Fold the paper along the lines and read the words.

Paste under the word bat.

hat

Patty Caterpillar

Example: Patty Caterpillar — hat — bat — fat — mat — pat — rat — sat

Short a
Level 3

COPYRIGHT © 1980 — THE LEARNING WORKS, INC.

38

Caterpillar

Paste under the word pat.

mat

fat

bat

sat

rat

pat

Short a
Level 3

COPYRIGHT © 1980 — THE LEARNING WORKS, INC.   39

Short e
Level 1

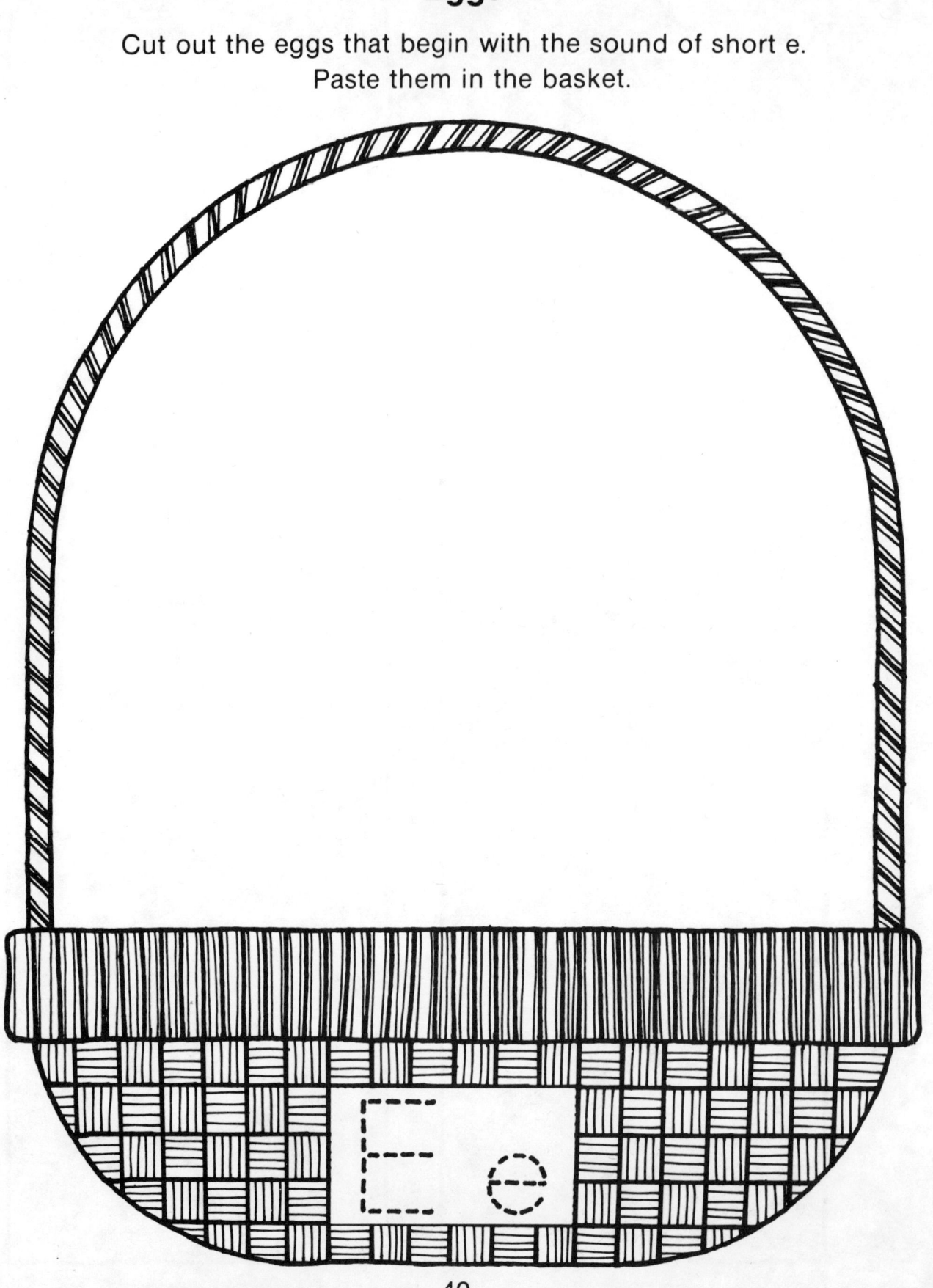

Eggs

Cut out the eggs that begin with the sound of short e.
Paste them in the basket.

Short e
Level 1

Eggs

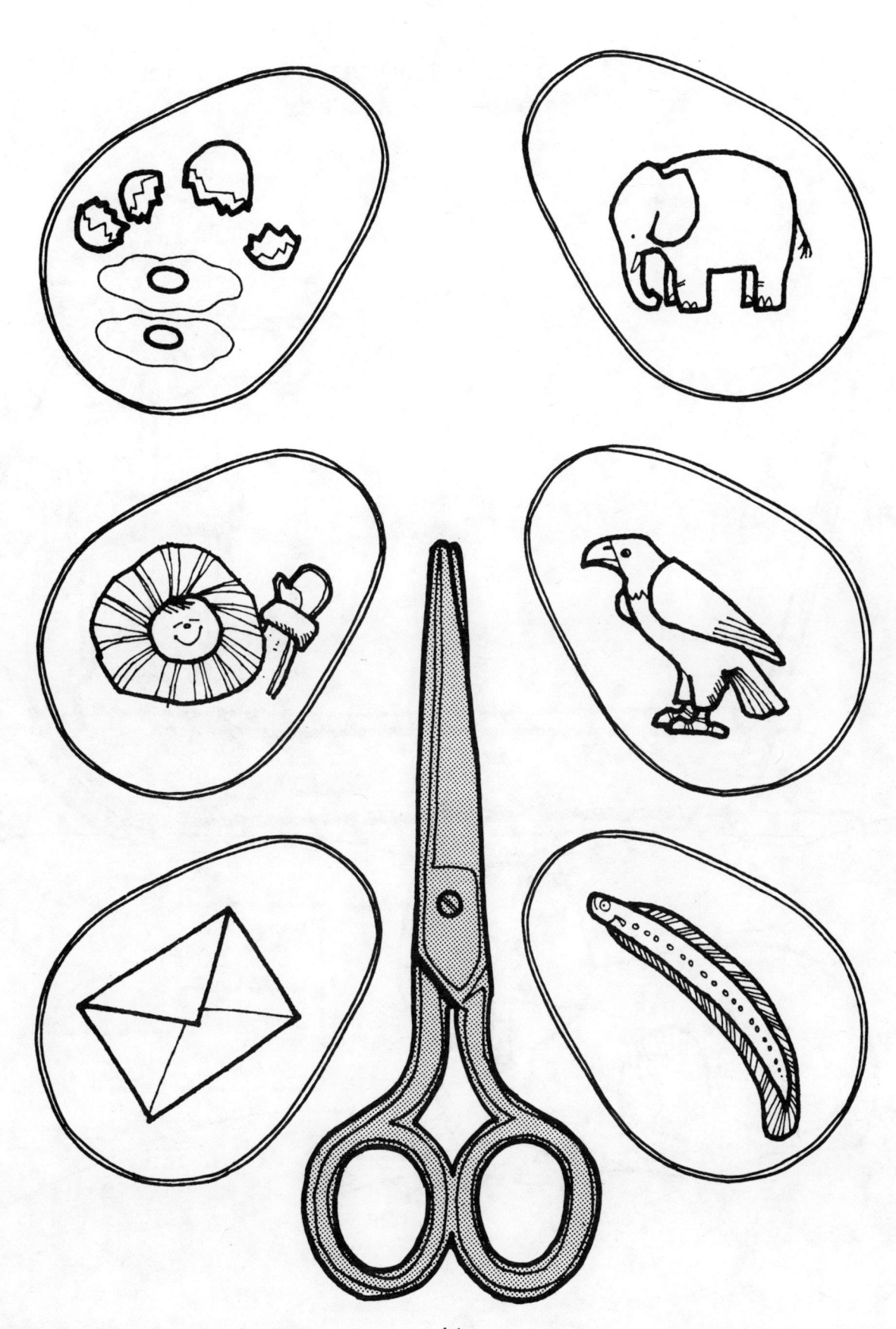

41

Short 3
Level 1

Eskimo

Cut out the packages that have the sound of short e.
Paste them in the sled.

Short e
Level 2

Eskimo

43

Jet

Cut out the jet. Cut out the wheel and attach it behind the jet with a brad. Turn the wheel and read the words.

Short e
Level 3

COPYRIGHT © 1980 — THE LEARNING WORKS, INC.

Short e
Level 3

Jet

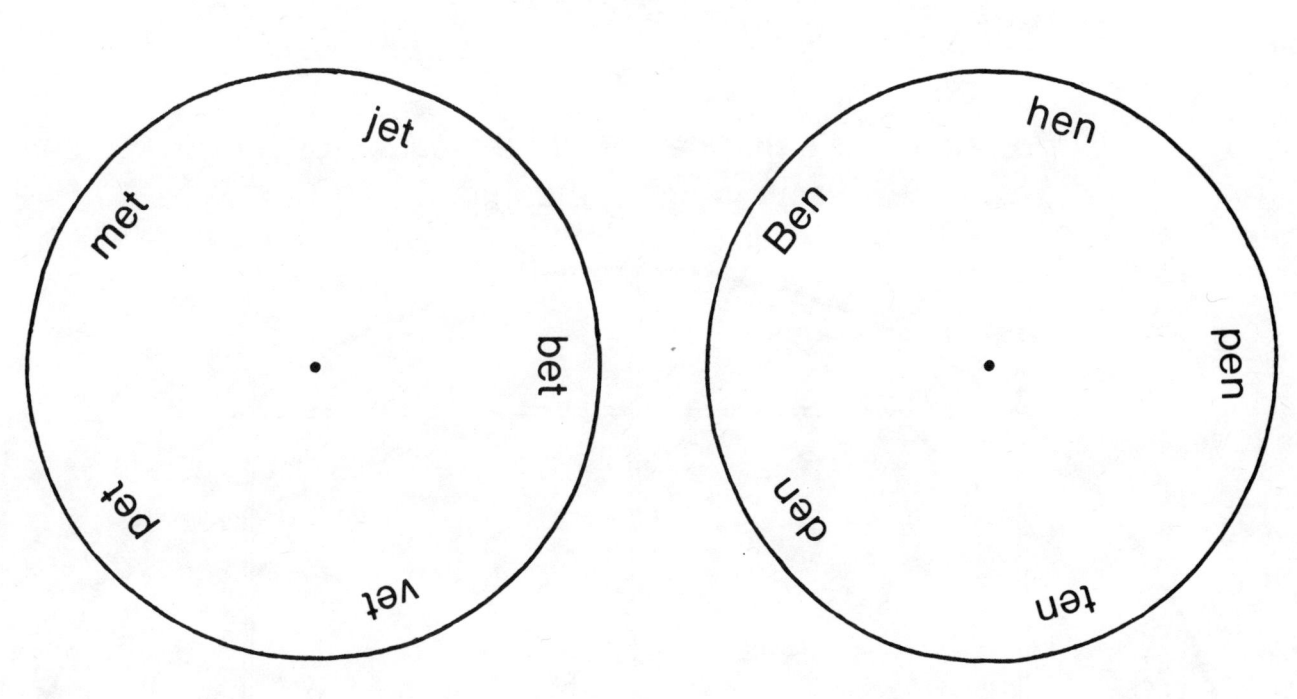

Spinner 1: jet, bet, vet, pet, met

Spinner 2: hen, pen, ten, den, Ben

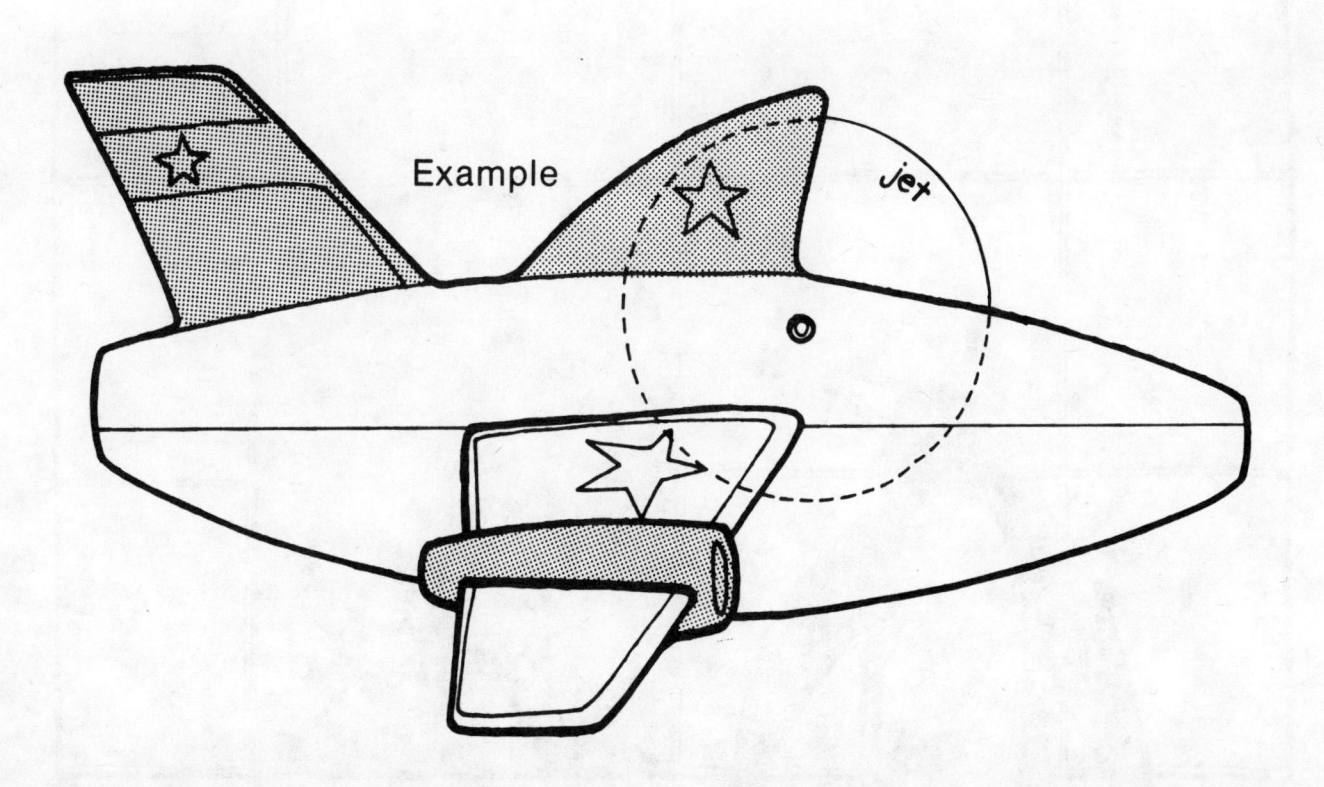

Example

Short i
Level 1

Igloo

Cut out the bricks that begin with the sound of short i.
Paste them on the igloo.

Short i
Level 1

Igloo

47

Short i
Level 2

Indian

Cut out the feathers that have the sound of short i.
Paste them on the Indian's headdress.

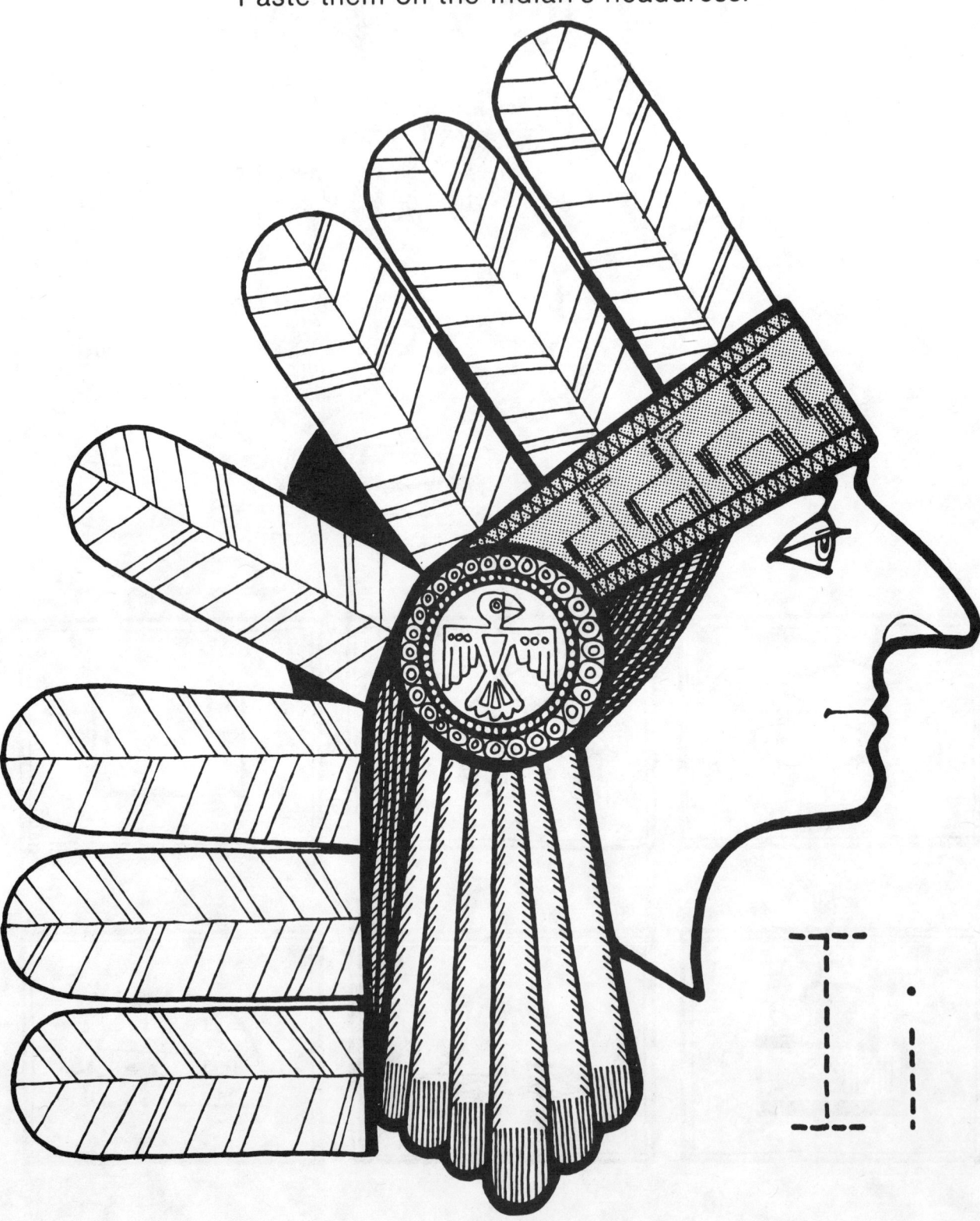

Short i
Level 2

Indian

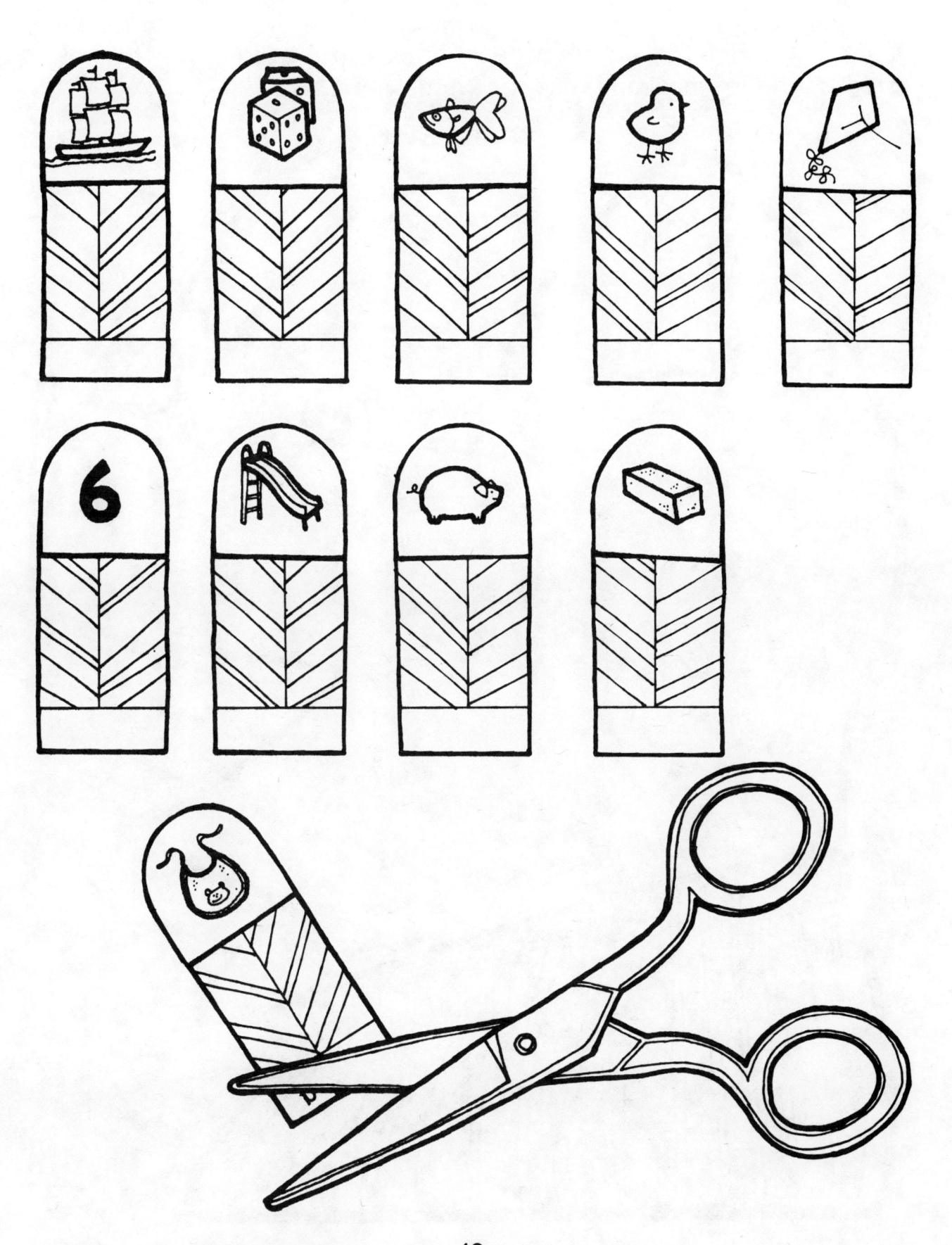

49

Short i
Level 3

Pig

Cut out Mr. Pig. Cut out the wheel and attach it behind Mr. Pig with a brad. Turn the wheel and read the words.

Short i
Level 3

Pig

Example

pin, bin, tin, spin, win, fin, kin

dig, twig, rig, wig, pig, fig, jig

51

COPYRIGHT © 1980 — THE LEARNING WORKS, INC.

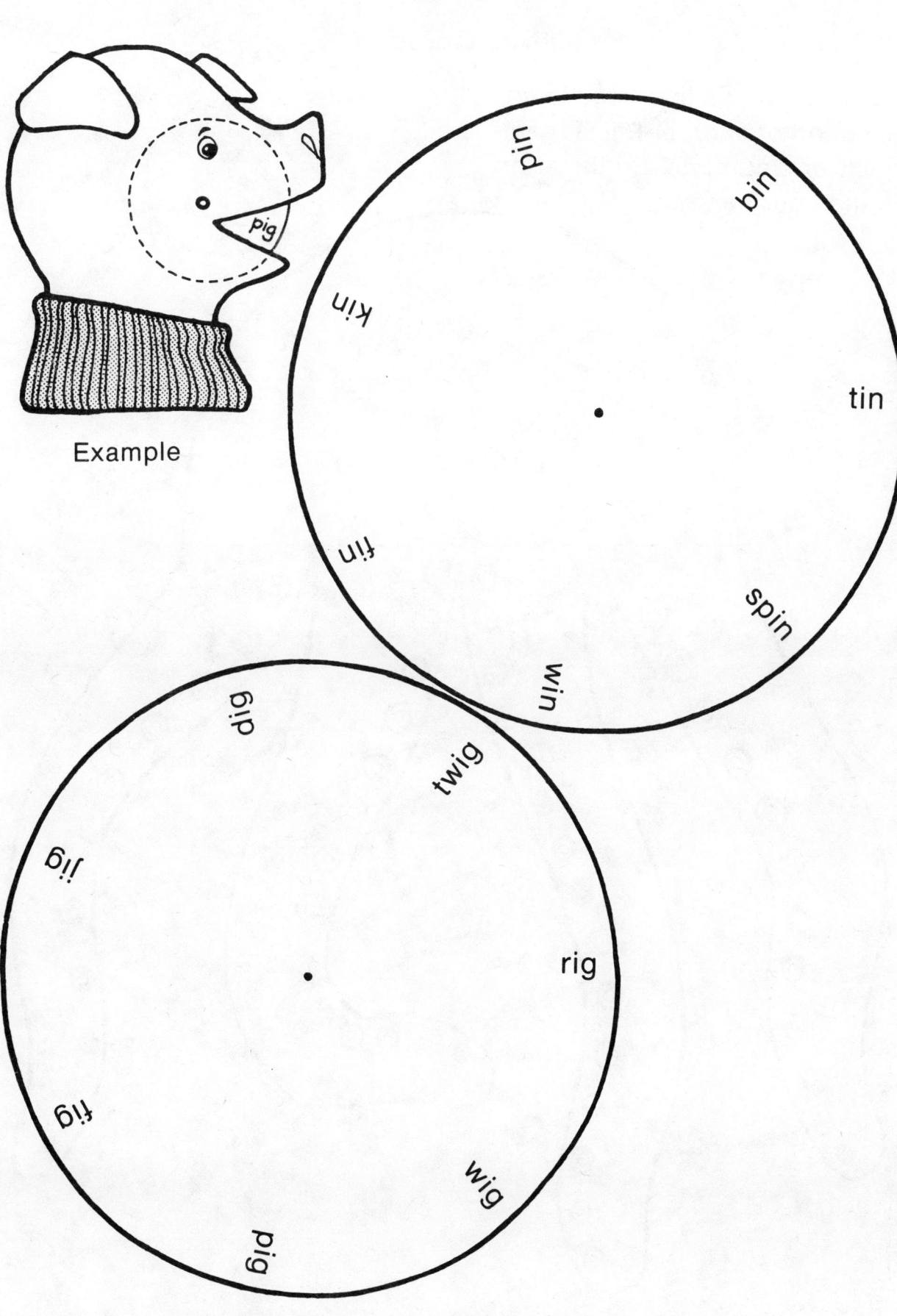

Short o
Level 1

Oliver Octopus

Cut out the arms that begin with the sound of short o. Paste them on Oliver Octopus. Curl the arms around your pencil.

Short o
Level 1

Oliver Octopus

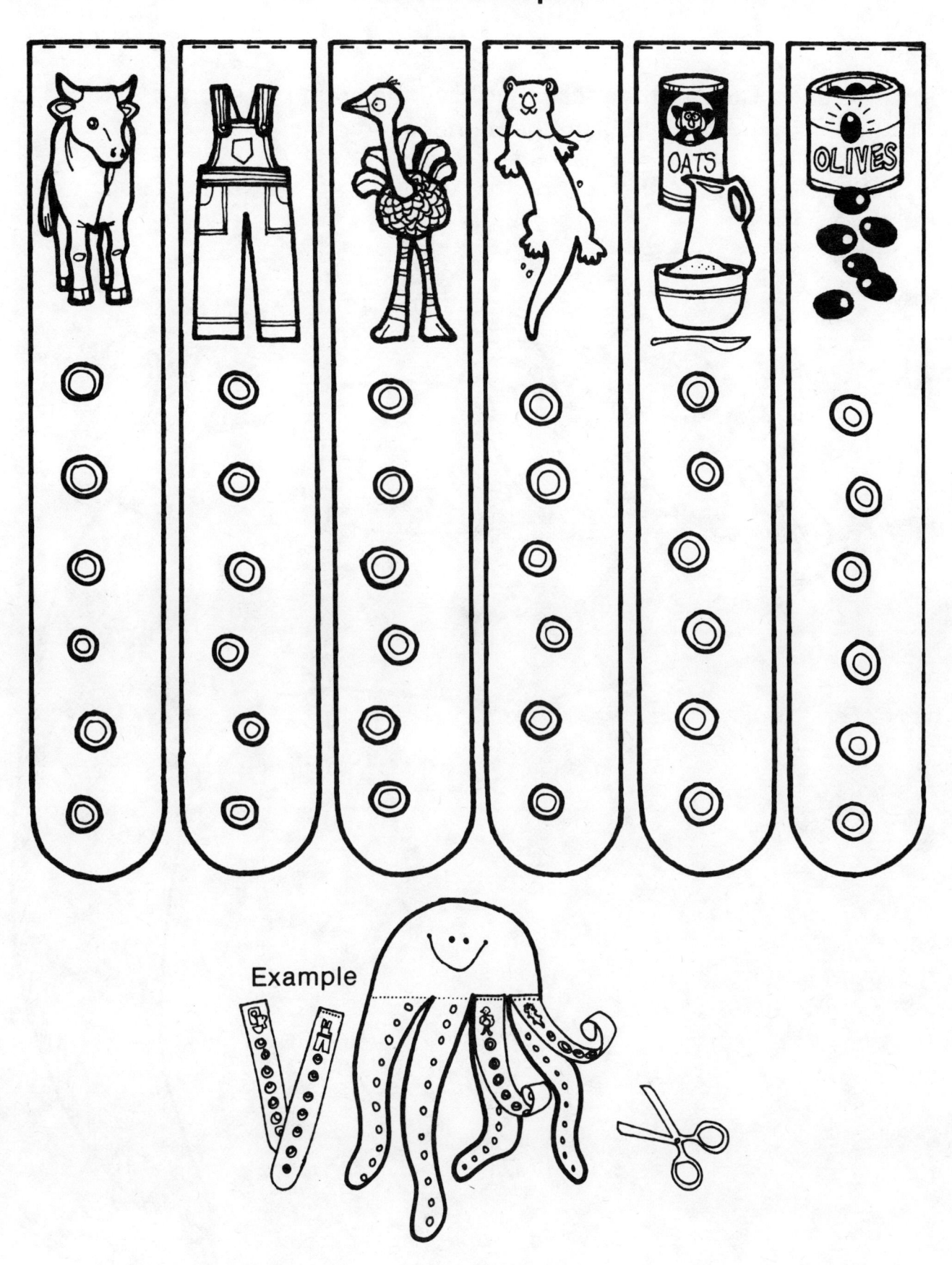

Example

53

Short o
Level 2

Otter

Cut out the rocks that have the sound of short o.
Paste them under the otter.

Short o
Level 2

Otter

Short o
Level 3

Frog on a Log

Cut out the list of words and fold them along the lines. Paste the first word in the frog's mouth to make a long tongue. Read the words.

Paste the word *frog* here.

Short o
Level 3

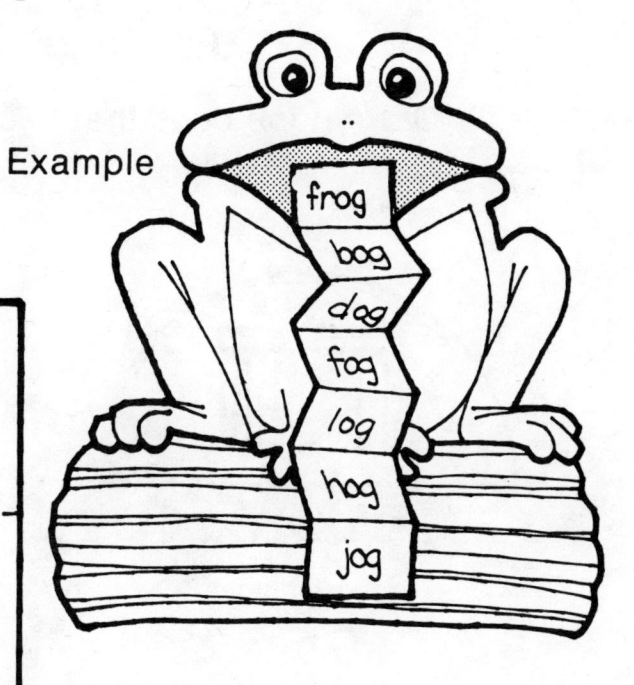

Frog

Example

frog	dock
bog	flock
dog	hock
fog	lock
log	rock
hog	sock
jog	tock

Short u
Level 1

Ugly Bugs Under Umbrella

Cut out the bugs that begin with the sound of short u.
Paste them under the umbrella.

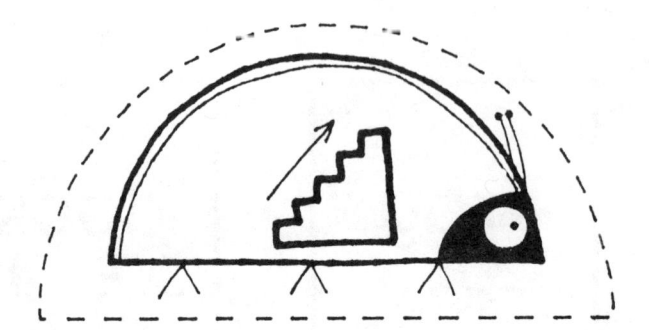

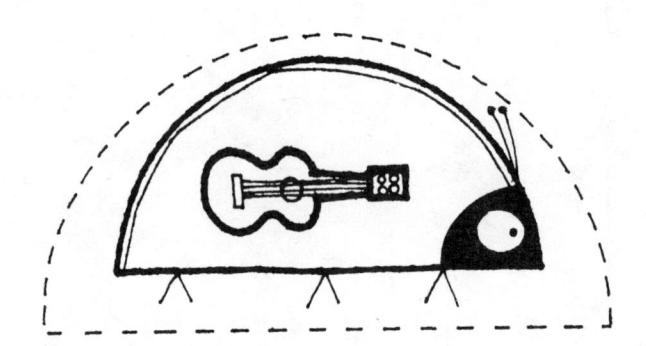

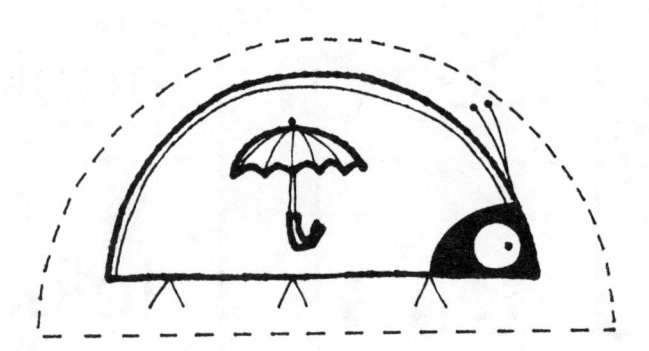

Short u
Level 1

Ugly Bugs Under Umbrella

Short u
Level 2

Muddy Ducks / Mud Puddle

Cut out the ducks that have the sound of short u.
Paste them in the mud puddle.

60

Short u
Level 2

Muddy Ducks / Mud Puddle

Uu

Short u
Level 3

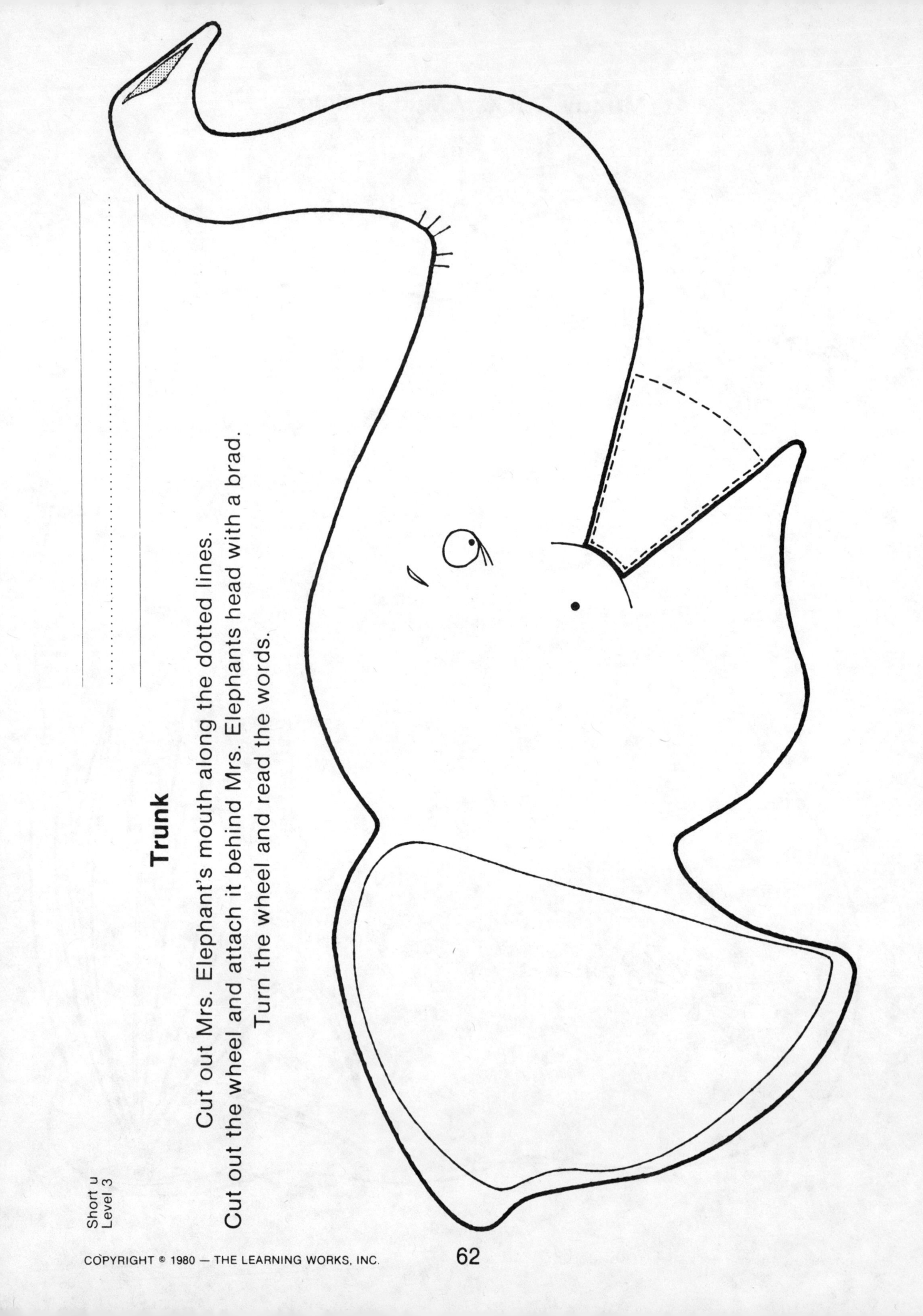

Trunk

Cut out Mrs. Elephant's mouth along the dotted lines.
Cut out the wheel and attach it behind Mrs. Elephants head with a brad.
Turn the wheel and read the words.

COPYRIGHT © 1980 — THE LEARNING WORKS, INC.

Short u
Level 3

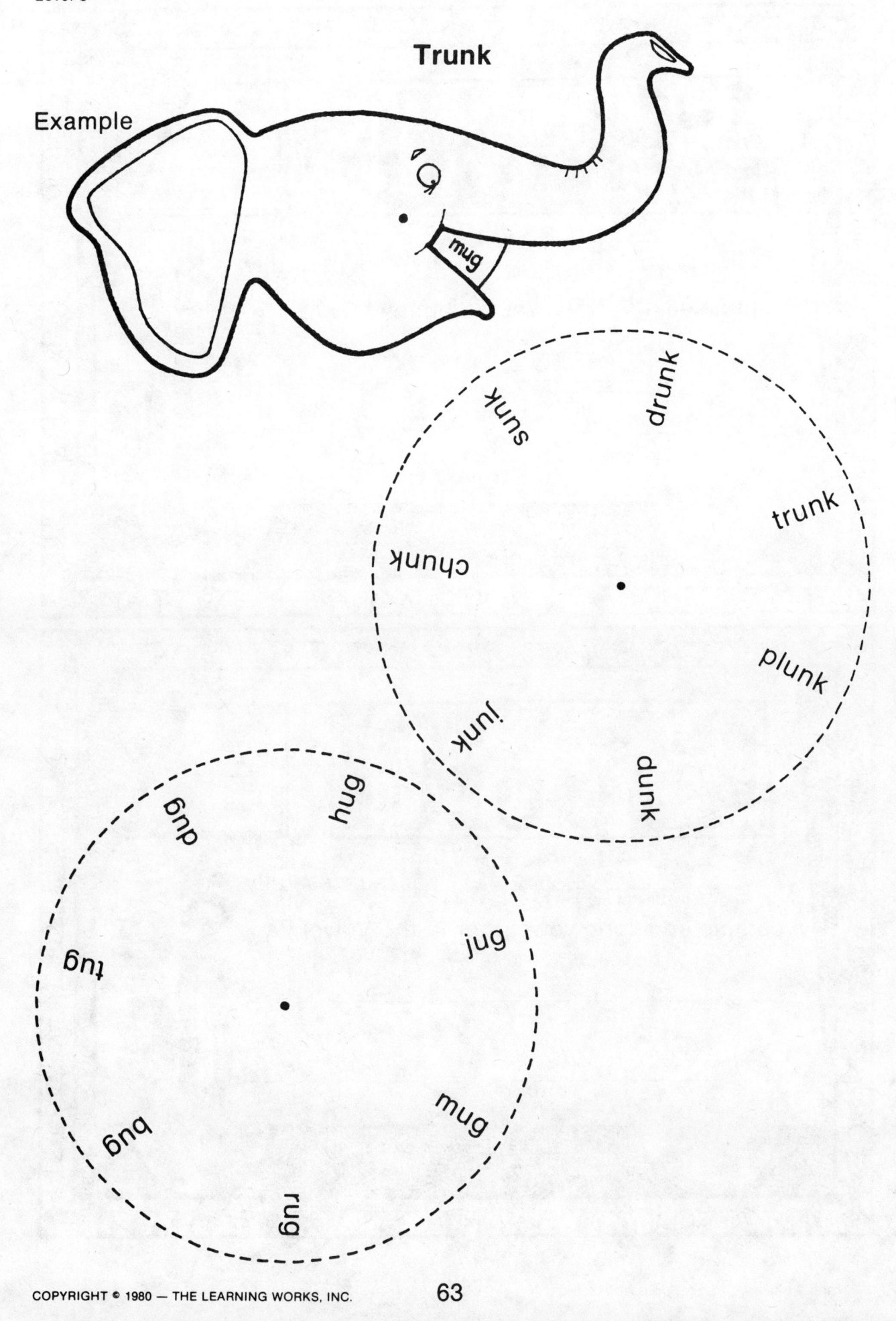

Trunk

Example

(elephant illustration with "mug" label)

Wheel 1 words: drunk, sunk, chunk, junk, dunk, plunk, trunk

Wheel 2 words: hug, dug, tug, bug, rug, mug, jug

COPYRIGHT © 1980 — THE LEARNING WORKS, INC.

AWARD

_____ has successfully
(Child's name)
completed a short vowel tour in the Vowel Van.

_____
(Teacher)

_____
(Date)

_____ has successfully
(Child's name)
completed a long vowel tour in the Vowel Van.

_____
(Teacher)

_____
(Date)

COPYRIGHT © 1980 — THE LEARNING WORKS, INC.

Art Ideas

The Vowel Caterpillar

Materials Needed: bottom halves of egg cartons, cut lengthwise into two strips
paint
paintbrushes
glue
sequins
pipe cleaners
small pictures representing vowel sounds being studied

Directions: Have children turn their carton strips upside down and then paint the top and sides. Allow time for the paint to dry. When the paint is dry, have children glue on sequin eyes and pipe cleaner antennae, which can be cut, curled, or rolled for effect. Then have them choose vowel pictures and glue them on the caterpillar's segments. Provide a time for children to share their vowel caterpillars.

Note: You may wish to limit the selection of vowel pictures to long or short vowels or to a single vowel sound.

Art Ideas

Vowel Flags

Materials Needed: construction paper cut into 6" x 9" rectangles with a vowel letter printed clearly in the upper left-hand corner.
12-inch oak tag strips, dowels, molding, or other lightweight pieces of wood to serve as flag supports
Magazine, brochure, or other pictures to represent vowel sounds
scissors
glue

Directions: From an assortment of pictures, have children choose ones to match the long or short sound of the vowel letter printed on their flags. Suggest they trim these pictures as needed and then glue them onto their flags in a montage. Display the finished flags for sharing.

The Vowel Hat

Materials Needed: 18" x 24" pieces of construction paper
crayons or marking pens
construction paper scraps
glue
stapler and staples or tape

Directions: Cut paper as shown and give each child a piece. Suggest children use crayons and marking pens or paper scraps and glue to decorate their hats to represent the vowel sound being studied. Pull straight edges around until lower curved edges meet. Then, tape or staple to make a cone-shaped hat. Plan a short (or long) vowels only menu, and wear the hats to a vowels party.

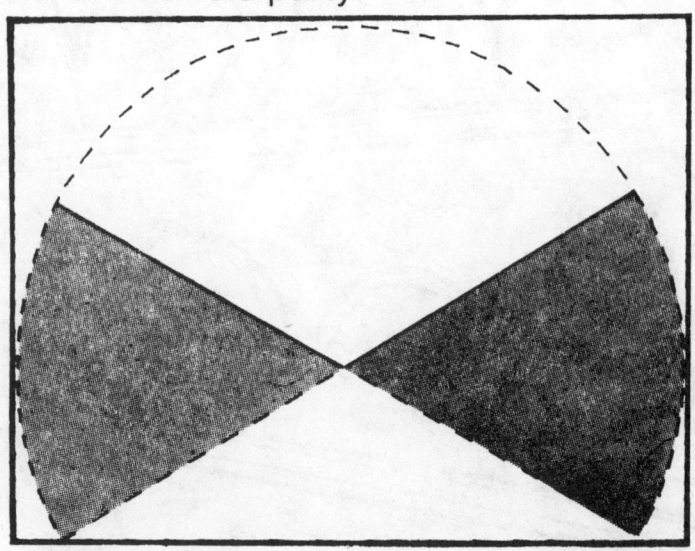

Cut along dotted line.

Shaded area shows approximate area of overlap.

Game Ideas

What's Inside?

Materials Needed: large bag
pictures representing vowel sounds

Directions: Put the pictures in the bag. In turn, each child reaches into the bag, draws out a picture, and names the vowel sound it suggests to him. If his answer is correct, he keeps the picture. The game ends when the bag is empty. The child who has collected the most pictures is the winner.

Note: If you intend to play the game often, you may wish to glue the vowel pictures to cards cut from tag board and to laminate them or cover then with clear contact paper.

Clap Your Hands

Materials Needed: large support picture to remind children of the vowel sound they are to listen for
list of words containing assorted vowel sounds, including the one you want to study
pictures illustrating this word list

Directions: Post the large support picture where all of the children can see it easily. Simultaneously show a picture and name the object pictured. Suggest that the children repeat the word after you say it. Tell them to clap their hands when they hear a vowel sound that matches the one suggested by the support picture.

Game Ideas

Bounce It, Say It

Materials Needed: ball

Directions: Have children sit in a semicircle facing you. Say a vowel and a word that contains it (for example, *a, apple*) and then bounce or roll the ball to one of the children. Tell the child to repeat your sound and word, say a new vowel sound and word, and then roll or bounce the ball back to you. Repeat the process around the semicircle or until all of the children have had at least one opportunity to catch, respond, and roll (or bounce).

Vowel Toss

Materials Needed: slant board with five large holes, each labeled for one of the main vowels
or
flat mat with circles drawn and marked for each of these vowels
three or four bean bags

Directions: Decide beforehand if the lesson is to be on long or short vowels and tell the children. In turn, players toss a bean bag, trying to get it in one of the holes or on one of the circles. When they succeed, they pronounce the sound of the vowel and name a word in which that sound appears.

Note: If children have trouble hitting the circles or holes, you may want to allow each turn to consist of multiple tosses, for example, three.

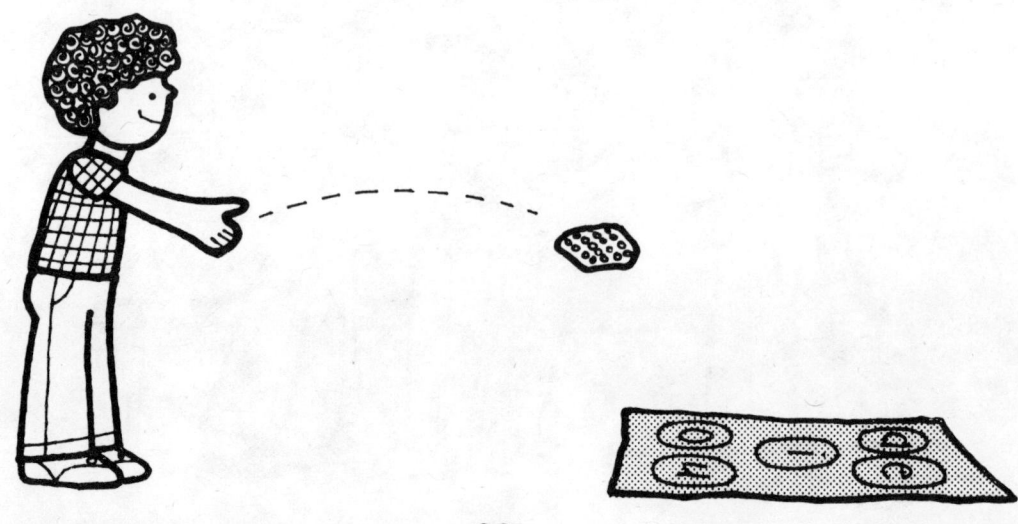

Game Ideas

Cross the Brook

Materials Needed: gray, tan, or brown tag board
marking pen
scissors

Preparation: Cut large (foot-sized) stone shapes out of tag. With the marking pen, print a vowel letter on each one.

Directions: Scatter the stone shapes on the floor. Explain to the children that the floor is a brook and that the shapes are stones on which they may cross without getting wet; however, only the stones marked with the vowel sound or sounds you name are safe. The others are too slippery, and stepping on them by mistake will cause a player to fall into the brook. Call out the vowel sound or show players a picture that represents the sound. For example, you might say, *"You may cross the brook only by stepping on the stones where you hear the a sound as in apple."* In turn, players then cross safely by stepping only on *A* or *a*.

Note: You may have all players take a turn for each vowel sound you name or call out a new vowel sound for each player in line.

Learning Center Ideas

Mail a Vowel to a Friend

Materials Needed:
vowel pictures
vowel stamps
envelopes
paste
class list
pencil
bag to be used as mail pouch

Preparation: Select and cut out vowel pictures. To make vowel stamps, use pinking shears to cut at least forty stamp-sized pieces of paper and print a vowel letter on each. Make the vowel pictures, stamps, and other materials needed available in a learning center.

Directions: Children using the center choose a picture and a stamp that goes with the sound the picture represents. They place the picture in an envelope and paste the stamp on the envelope. Then, consulting the class list, they address the "letter" to a classmate and place it in the mail pouch to be delivered at the end of reading time.

Note: The child who receives the "letter" can benefit from "reading" the picture to see if it matches the stamp. Encourage verbal communication.

Supermarket

Materials Needed: 5 large shopping bags labeled *a e i o u*
many empty containers (boxes, cartons, or cans) of foods whose names start with or include the vowel sounds being studied

Directions: Tell children using the center to sort food items into the correct shopping bag. Explain whether they are to listen for and sort by long or short vowel sounds.

Suggested Foods:

For Long Vowels		For Short Vowels	
apricots	ice cream	apples	egg plant
cake	pineapple	apple butter	chips
raisins	rice	applesauce	popsicles
peaches	oatmeal	cabbage	olives
peas	fruit	ham	butter
beans	juice	jam	gum
beets	prunes	eggs	muffins
seeds			

Learning Center Ideas

Peek and Spell

Materials Needed: several large pictures representing one vowel sound (for example, *a* in *cap, hat, mat, cat, ham*)
glue
construction paper or tag board
marking pen
large container of letters or letter cards
large pocket chart

Preparation: Glue each picture to a piece of tag board or construction paper. On the back of each, print the word that names the pictured object. Laminate each picture or cover it with clear contact paper.

Directions: The child selects a picture, puts the picture in the pocket, and uses letters to spell the word the picture represents. She is allowed to peek behind the picture to help her remember the word or to check her spelling of it.

Picture Words

Materials Needed: assorted pictures representing short vowels in the medial position
tag board cut into 2" x 2" squares and 2" x 6" strips
marking pen

Preparation: To make a set of vowel letter cards, print one vowel letter on each 2" x 2" tag square. To make a set of word cards, glue a picture in the middle of each 2" x 6" strip and then print the beginning and ending letters needed to spell the pictured word. Laminate both sets of cards or cover them with clear contact paper.

Directions: The child looks at each word card, decides which medial vowel sound is represented by the picture in the middle, and places the appropriate vowel letter card over the picture to make a word and spell the name of the pictured object.

Bulletin Board Ideas

Vowel Vans

Materials Needed: large cutout shape of the vowel van for each child
magazines
scissors
paste

Directions: Children select and cut out magazine pictures that represent the vowel sound(s) being studied. Then, they paste the pictures on the vans. Display the vans on a bulletin board and provide a sharing time.

The Vowel Van Tour

Materials Needed: pocket chart
five vowel vans labeled *a e i o u*
assorted vowel picture cards

Preparation: To make vowel picture cards, glue pictures representing vowel sounds on tag board cards cut to a standard size that is large enough to hold the picture but small enough to fit easily in the chart pocket.

Directions: The child arranges the five vowel vans across the top of the pocket chart and then sorts the pictures by placing each one under the correct vowel van.

Variation: Use vowel word cards instead of vowel picture cards to encourage the child to focus on the medial position of the vowel letter.